Bending the Bow

Bending the Bow

An Anthology of African Love Poetry

Edited by Frank M. Chipasula

Southern Illinois University Press
Carbondale

21 20 19 18   5 4 3 2

Library of Congress Cataloging-in-Publication Data
Bending the bow : an anthology of African love poetry
/ edited by Frank M. Chipasula.
    p. cm.
  Some poems originally written in English,
French, and Portuguese, some translated from
various African languages.
  Includes bibliographical references.
  ISBN-13: 978-0-8093-2842-0 (alk. paper)
  ISBN-10: 0-8093-2842-9 (alk. paper)
  1. Love poetry, African (English) 2. Love poetry,
African—Translations into English. I. Chipasula,
Frank Mkalawile.
  PR9346.B46 2009
  821'.00803543096—dc22   2008052583

Printed on recycled paper. ♻

for my late parents
                out of whose love . . .
Pat, Helen, and Masauko,
                without whose love . . .
and also for you all
                my brothers and sisters,
                whose love . . .

Enrich the world,
Make it beautiful;
And when you are gone,
Let the earth miss you.

Contents

Acknowledgments

A Judge William Holmes Cook Professorship at Southern Illinois University, Carbondale freed me to devote a great deal of time to refining the anthology. Also, funds from the professorship kept me well supplied with the materials that ensured the book's publication. I thank the offices of the dean of the College of Liberal Arts and of the provost for the nomination and appointment. I also thank my friend, Dr. Teresa Barnes, who came to my aid when I needed help contacting a poet in Cape Town, South Africa. The following scholars lent the words for "love" in their languages: Dr. Nkonko Kamwangamalu, renowned linguist and friend; Dr. Onuchekwa Jemie, former colleague at Howard University; and Mr. Moses Okeyo at Idaho State University, Pocatello. Of all my many cheerleaders, Pat was always right behind my back pushing me to finish the work; Barbara and Larry did the same from the morning side of the country; while Helen and Masauko kept wondering when they would stop hearing about this new anthology.

Bending the Bow

Introduction: The African Names of Love

If the Egyptians were the inventors of the love-poem, and it is that, with their love of brightness and gaiety, they were, we may well regard it as one of their chief contributions to literature. . . . [I]t may safely be affirmed that up to the present no poet has written of love without saying many things which his Egyptian fore-runners thought and said three thousand years ago.

—T. Eric Peet

> It is stronger than my reason,
> it is stronger than my soul,
> I am ashamed of it, but I can neither resist nor hide my disease.
> This is why I am telling you my deadly secret.
>
> —from "Love Defeats Queen Saran"

> You have beautiful flesh
> You have beautiful legs
> You have beautiful arms
> All of you is beautiful
> You have done beautiful things, you have done beautiful
>   things, girl, you have done beautiful things
>
> —from "Encouraging a Dancer"

Bending the Bow extends the parameters of African poetry into an area that has hitherto been neglected and marginalized in order to afford the reader a fuller appreciation of African literature, which has been dominated by overtly political themes and texts. It constitutes an archaeological effort aimed at reclaiming and reinstating into African literary discourse a poetic genre that is indigenous to Africa, having been invented in ancient Egypt, a fact many Egyptologists have asserted over the years. It exposes the reader to a diverse and varied body of love poetry, an important dimension that has until now been missing from the literature.

Arranged in three sections, this anthology demonstrates the development of love poetry in Africa from its origins in the anonymously written Egyptian love poems of the New Kingdom, which predate the biblical love poetry of King Solomon by over two thousand years, through the oral traditions of sung love poetry, to a showcase of modern and contemporary written love poetry in a continuum of performance that testifies to the genre's longevity and endurance.

Love poetry's earliest manifestations are in the lyrical poetry of the New Kingdom, which boasts a written tradition in hieroglyphic script. These love poems from the Eighteenth through Twentieth Dynasties of the New Kingdom (roughly from 1300 to 1100 B.C.), which predate Homer by half a millennium, vividly evoke aspects of ancient Egyptian society, documenting for us courtship practices, young lovers' romantic trysts masked as bird-catching in the reeds along the Nile, and the penchant for feasts, festivals, and merry-making that characterized that civilization. The poetry depicts a society that prized affluence and gloried in good cheer, though we often associate it with a chronic preoccupation with death and the afterlife, owing perhaps to the popularity of the mummies. Further, the core imagery in these same love songs informs the Song of Songs, one of the world's greatest love poems, whose central metaphors, dominant imagery, and symbols betray the poem's derivation from African love songs and wedding songs.

While these poems project a spectrum of emotions, they are first and foremost celebrations of youthful unmarried love, expressions of desire for physical union with the beloved, and optimistic projections of that love into a harmonious marital future. Though driven by an intense desire for sexual intercourse with their loved ones, the lovers are often quite discreet, sneaking up to their beloveds' houses veiled in darkness and entering through windows, or employing subterfuge and chicanery to win over their intended lovers. In a considerable number of the Cairo love songs, we hear lovers' calls as the young people arrange secret trysts in the reeds by the Nile or in enclosed gardens, where the personified sycamore trees and birds are secret-sharers who promise reticence over the dalliances they witness, while others, favored by Hathor, the goddess of love, exclaim their joy at the return of a lover. However, the fact that these young lovers are secretive about their affairs and must keep their activities out of reach of their parents suggests parental disapproval of premarital sex in ancient Egypt. This is still the case in many traditional African societies, where sexuality is regulated by a complex set of taboos and their attendant punitive measures.

However, these sung love poems do not always depict individualized lovers, for quite often during the Eighteenth Dynasty and the Ramesside periods, they served as entertainment or diversion at banquets and festivities. The love songs fueled the party mood and license that permitted erotic expression, inspired in part by the presence of beautiful attendants who regaled the guests with wreaths, fragrant oils, and food and drink, urging them, on behalf of their masters, to drink excessively and to enjoy themselves fully. Thus, these sung and danced poems realized their full potential in the larger social context of good cheer, merry-making, hospitality, and ostentatious gift-giving. Apparently, within this context of relaxed morality and lasciviousness, taboos could be broken, if only in sung poetry.

Structurally, this poetry reveals a sophistication in composition that rivals its modern and contemporary counterparts. Its preference for simple diction, unrhymed lines, and variety of line length as well as its colloquial language and cadence of the speaking voices, for instance, reflect its affinities with the essential qualities of modernist verse. The conversational tone of these poems also reveals the intimacy of personal and private speech, the language of lovers, which retains its verve even today.

Powerfully erotic, the poetry portrays young women who unabashedly pursue their love objects as they express their desire for sexual union, as in the poem, "Love, How I'd Love to Slip Down to the Pond," in which a young woman entices her lover to go and swim with her so that she may show him her "red fish" while she bewitches him with her beauty through her sheer, wet, clinging linen swimsuit, inflaming him with the following suggestive words:

> But then I'd say softer,
>   eyes bright with your seeing:
>   A gift, love. No words.
>   Come closer and
>   look, it's all me.

Thus, through these love songs, ancient Egypt has bequeathed to us the legacy of a healthy eroticism bursting out of energetic bodies that appear youthful more than three and half thousand years later. What the ancient teenage lovers expressed with so much boldness, candor, and eloquence reaches us today through the echoes in the metaphorical and euphemism-laden *taarab* songs of the Swahili coast. Indeed, we have to project ourselves back into the past to encounter the precursors to the questing or pining lovers of later romantic poetry. Even the notion of love as an incurable yet pleasant malady, which dominates much of Swahili love poetry, for instance, makes its first appearance here.

From these ancient love songs, a natural progression leads to the second section, which offers a rich, though not exhaustive, sampling of contemporary dance songs, courtship songs, and wedding songs as well as other love songs from the continent's diverse ethnicities that reveal the rhythmic pulse of traditional Africa. Since the African village is a highly yet subtly eroticized environment, only those expatriates whose contacts with Africans are limited to superficial interactions with house servants will be excused for being blind to the love transactions that occur before their own eyes. Here, in abundance, is incontrovertible evidence against the assertions by some respectable African critics who have declared emphatically the dearth of love poetry in Africa, quite unwittingly confirming the colonial doubts regarding the Africans' humanity. Assailed by a rare and acute type of deafness, these august scholars have yet to hear love in *bolingo*, a Lingala term for both "love" and "beloved" that has crossed mountains and oceans with Congolese Soukous music. For more than five thousand years, the Amazigh people of the Grand Atlas Mountains, whose name means "free or noble," though the Arabs called them Berber, or Barbarians, have expressed various versions of *tayri* (love) for one another in Tamazight, a very old African language. Other African names of love include *ohole* (OshiNdonga); *chikondi* (love) and *chikondano* (reciprocal love) (ChiNyanja); *dinanga* (TshiLuba); *ife* (Yoruba); *ihunanya* (Igbo); *lolo* (Ewe); *pendo, mapendo, mapenzi, mahaba, huba, nyonda,* and *upendano* (mutual love) (KiSwahili); *rudo* and *chido* (ChiShona); *hera* (Luo/Dholuo); *urukundo* (kiRundi); *thando* (SiNdebele, isiZulu); *ukutemwa* (IciBemba); *chitemwa* (ChiTumbuka); and *lerato* (Sesotho). The frequency with which these terms appear in African songs testifies to the centrality of the love theme in traditional African poetry.

The Acoli love songs, though not unique, deserve special mention because of their great impact on Okot p'Bitek, one of Africa's greatest twentieth-century poets, who gathered and translated them. His exemplary archival work and rendering of traditional sung poems in English helped to inaugurate a new poetic movement in East Africa during the 1960s. His slim volume, *Horn of My Love*, bequeathed to African literature an important treasure trove of faithfully translated Acoli love songs that retain their particular flavor, even in English. In his introduction, p'Bitek pays homage to the composers of these beautiful, sometimes bawdy courtship songs sung during the Larakaraka (or Orak) dance. Since the purpose of these dances is to enable the suitors to conduct successful courtship, the singers and dancers must display their unique skills in the arena. Performed at night, under showers of moonlight, these extremely licentious courtship dances liberate the youthful singer-lovers into making overt allusions to the sweetness of lovemaking in order to break down their potential lovers' bashfulness and to facilitate the initiation of love relations that must develop into marriage.

Similarly, a modern poetic movement in Madagascar, Africa's largest island, owes its genesis to an old traditional form of courtship poetry that has flourished over centuries. *Hain-teny*, the "formal" Malagasy classical dialogue love poetry, animates and fertilizes the love poems of such prominent Negritude poets as Jean-Joseph Rabéarivelo and Flavien Ranaivo, who consciously experimented with these oral poetic forms as a base for modern poetry. Rabéarivelo's translations, renderings, and interpretations of *hain-teny*, published as *Vieilles chansons des pays d'Imerina* in 1939, availed to French readers a rich body of dramatic courtship songs in which the lovers engage in a protracted, lyrical question-answer dialogue, which constitutes a test of the lovers' commitment. His compatriot Ranaivo also profitably exploited the rich poetic resources of the *hain-teny*, thus rooting and anchoring his poetry in the folk culture that gave it its authenticity.

Initially, the Malagasy poetry appeared to suggest structural possibilities for the third section, which showcases diverse modern and contemporary written love poetry, and thus presented me with unique problems of arrangement. Superficially, the logical order would have been to match a poem with its cultural antecedent in the preceding section, which would have been limiting, considering that both modern and contemporary African poets have often sought their literary models beyond the clan and tribe. Also, by placing northern and southern poets side by side, I have preempted the tendency among certain readers to tally offerings as a way of determining an editor's idiosyncrasies, proclivities, biases, or assumed judgment of literary worth. I have also opted for the present arrangement in order to demonstrate the existence of subtle literary exchanges among African poets over millennia, the cross-fertilization between the poetry composed along the Nile, the Horn of Africa, and the Swahili Coast being a case in point.

Swahili poetry owes its birth to seventeenth-century poet Liyongo Fumo, a great pillar of both Swahili society and literature. Liyongo, who died around 1690, introduced into Swahili poetry the erotic *gungu* songs that accompanied wedding dances, whose impact on the literature has persisted into the contemporary period. These songs are celebrations of many aspects of love, both romantic and marital, and were sung to enliven wedding ceremonies and festivities. Another significant literary figure among the Swahili is the great Muyaka bin Haji (al Ghassaniy), a wealthy and politically powerful citizen of Mombasa, Kenya. Muyaka was the leading poet of the Swahili language whose poetry left a permanent mark on succeeding generations of the coastal poets. A successful businessman who owned a fleet of ships, his marine imagery and metaphorical reference to his first wife as his beloved vessel reveal these coastal people's preoccupation with seafaring and transoceanic trade with the islands off the East African coast and the Middle East as a source of their affluence and their literary models.

Despite these viable traditions of love poetry in Africa, contemporary written African literature has so entrenched overtly political protest poetry that one actually *expects* it from an African poet. The tragic consequence has been the stagnation and predictability of contemporary African poetry. All the same, a few seemingly political poets have also crafted memorable verses fusing politics and love. Among Léopold Sédar Senghor's Negritude poems, for instance, are some of the most beautiful love lyrics couched in praises of the *signare*, a class of noble Senegalese women. One of the most powerful, passionate, and intensely erotic poems in this anthology is David Diop's "Rama Kam." Spare and sparse, the poem is a celebration of the poet's wife, Virginie Kamara, and projects the woman as natural, beautiful, and extremely sexually desirable. Frank and bold, the poem depicts their lovemaking as the very essence and source of life:

> When you love Rama Kam
> A tornado quivers

In the lightning night of your flesh
And leaves me full of the breath of you

The images of the quivering tornado, the bolt of lightning, the exchange of intense erotic energy—breath and life itself between the lovers—lend power to the poem. Diop is not unique in his portrayal of his loving wife as nurturing. Love poetry in many African cultures exists as praise songs in which the singer-lover extols the loved one's physical and spiritual attributes and virtues. Praise singers imagine their lovers in idyllic and idealistic ways in ancient Egyptian love songs, in Swahili, in Shona, and in other poetic traditions, all of which shore up this aspect of the sung love poem.

The traditional belief that the love song is an exclusively male genre because men must conduct courtship, an important prelude to marriage, begs reconsideration. Many African folk traditions are rich repositories of women's love songs that continue to empower contemporary women poets to write some of the most ardently erotic and intensely spiritual love poetry. Ifi Amadiume's work, for instance, testifies eloquently to African women poets' accomplishments in this area. Her love poems are simultaneously sensual and sensuous as well as boldly erotic, as in "Show Me All" and "Dubem's Patience," whose personae are versed in Igbo folk philosophy and are comfortable with their sexuality. Her treatment of the sexual act as a necessary nourishment further confirms the African people's healthy attitude toward sexuality that Naana Banyiwa Horne also celebrates in "*Sore Ka Pra*: Whoopie, Akan Time," a poem that depicts the healthy everyday eroticism of Akan folk life in the sexually fulfilled women who exude sensuality and rejoice in genuine love as an important aspect of their existence in traditional African societies.

All the same, from what some of the poets tell us, it has not always been easy to love in Africa, but in some instances love has managed to triumph over the hurdles in its path. Adam Small's ballad of the tragic love between Diana, a white girl, and Martin, a black boy, in apartheid South Africa tells of love's supremacy over artificially erected racial barriers. How many such interracial love affairs ended this way in South Africa, we will never know. However, love empowers the couple to defy "de Lô" to the very end:

Said Diana, said Martin
What Lô?
God's Lô
man's Lô
devil's Lô
what Lô

Clearly, love empowers them to choose imprisonment over obedience to an unjust "devil's Lô" that hinders human communion. They achieve victory in defeat when they commit suicide rather than submit to the irrational Immorality Act as an ultimate act of defiance of apartheid.

In "Love in a Season of Terror," Niyi Osundare's lovers must persevere and survive military dictatorship and violence as corrupt leaders place roadblocks in the path of human development. Corpses, flying mortar shells unleashed by drunken generals, lethal weapons, and utter terror separate two distanced lovers who yearn for physical union. Unfortunately for the two, the bayonet between the general's legs proves too powerful for the lovers, and they can never hope for intimacy as long as he is in power.

The often reckless and dismissive pronouncements by eminent African literary scholars regarding the paucity of love poetry in Africa have negatively persuaded international readers to regard the continent's poetry as basically political. This possibly explains the absence of African love poems from "international" love poetry anthologies. A great deal of the blame must be placed at the door of certain African scholars whose claims that love poetry is a "rare species" in Africa may have unduly discouraged editors from seeking contributions from African poets. For instance, although in her introduction to Jean Garrigue's anthology *Love Poems*, Nancy Sullivan claims that love's "landscape is international," not a single contribution from Africa appears in the book (xxxv). Could this be an accidental oversight, or the result of the writer's conviction that Africans are not composers of love poetry? "From the civilization of the Lower Nile to that of the Lower Hudson, more poets have written more convincingly, more poignantly about love than about any other subject," claims the blurb for Jon Stallworthy's contribution to the genre, *A Book of Love Poetry*, an Oxford University Press reissue of *The Penguin Book of Love Poetry*, yet "the civilization of the Lower Nile" has been completely overlooked in the anthology. Surprisingly, only one poet with some African connection, though she may not be an African, is featured in Wendy Mulford's anthology, *Love Poems by Women: An Anthology of Poetry from Around the World and Through the Ages*. With three assistant editors involved in the project and such an inclusive subtitle, one would think that they would have found more love poems from Africa.

Could the problem lie with the editors' narrow and exclusionary definition of love that easily precludes Africa? Yet the definition of love by Jon Stallworthy hardly explains why he bypassed a whole continent, considering the availability of ancient Egyptian love poems as well as more recent crystals of folk love songs that precede his anthology. I am reluctant to accept that since Stallworthy roots his definition in the old Indo-European tongues, his reach is necessarily as constricted as the following assertion may seem to suggest: "Love [Old English *lufu*, Indo-European *leubh*, from the same root as the Sanskrit *lubh*, to desire] of the Beloved accounts for many of the most intense moments in most lives; moments generating the emotion that, recollected in tranquility, may crystallize into poems" (19). He raised my expectations further regarding the contents of his own anthology with the following statement: "Before ever man learnt to make graphic symbols of his sounds, he had his love songs as well as his war songs and his reaping songs" (21). Since all these sung poetries that Stallworthy enumerates have been present in Africa, it is perhaps not without justification that we would wonder about the absence of African love songs from his anthology. Fortunately, Jan Knappert has carefully documented some of the most beautiful African love songs in his anthologies of Swahili poetry, *A Choice of Flowers: Chaguo la Maua: An Anthology of Swahili Love Poetry* and *Four Centuries of Swahili Verse*.

By *bending the bow*, I challenge African poets to seize this musical instrument that they might play on it the love songs that accompany gift-giving among people in order to heal the breaches among us and offer us the possibility of achieving wholeness once again. Historically, African oral poets as mediators in conflicts have sung their strife-torn societies into order, quite often utilizing the bow because of its versatility as a weapon, hunting implement, and instrument for creating life-giving, life-affirming art that constitutes the essential glue in human bonds. Legendary Somali poets mediated in clan conflicts, cooling flaming hearts with their songs, no matter how irreconcilable the differences appeared to be between the warring clans. Are contemporary African poets singing love enough to perform similar peace-keeping roles? In 1956, Swahili poet Juma Bhalo made the following claim about love:

> Love is a wall
> which will stop war;
> they will not persist in discord
> who love consciously.

Considering that love of kin rather than discord once enabled us to build strong communities, the internecine pogroms in Africa are sometimes quite hard to comprehend. Isn't love the mother of genuine solidarity?

Every African community or ethnic group has a treasure trove of sung or chanted love poems, some of which have been written down since the discovery of papyrus and the invention of writing in Egypt. What is certain, however, is that because readers and scholars have persistently focused on political poetry, they have almost totally ignored and marginalized love poems while simultaneously making seemingly authoritative yet uninformed, fallacious statements about the lack of love poetry in Africa. The assertion that love poetry is rare in Africa is especially troubling, coming as it does from African literary scholars who grew up in African villages listening to or even singing these love songs they could not recognize as poetry, most likely because no Westerner had validated them.

Love, a construction of the human intellect, distinguishes us from and elevates us above other beings. The conventions and rules governing love transactions between lovers may vary from one culture to another, yet the major features of those manners are the same. And while the names of love may be myriad, the human affliction they describe has not spared many Africans.

When I began this journey quite a few rains ago, I did not set out with any preconceptions of African love poetry. From the outset, I was willing to accept a wide-open definition of love, which this anthology reflects. In one case, an Eritrean master of the poetic riddle, Reesom Haile, seduces us with a plethora of unabashedly erotic metaphors as he confesses his obsession with his favorite mistress (indeed, whose shameless daughter would allow herself to be taken any time and anywhere like that?): coffee. Haile's witty and brazen poem suggests the immense natural metaphorical properties of the riddle and its limitless possibilities for the daring modern African poet willing to experiment with folk poetic forms in the work of renewal that awaits our indigenous literatures. The riddle is omnipresent in traditional Africa; here lies the rich ore that awaits the African image-maker's patient hands.

Finally, this anthology in no way pretends to be comprehensive, though it has been distilled from a massive body of work. Considering Africa's size and cultural diversity, any such work would be cumbersome and pose extraordinary challenges to its editor. The present anthology is merely a sampling of the rich sung and written traditions of African love poetry hitherto neglected by editors of international love poetry anthologies. I hope that henceforth, editors will heed Nancy Sullivan's claim that love's "landscape is international, its concerns timeless" and thereby enrich their books with contributions from Africa, the birthplace of both humanity and love poetry.

Selected Bibliography

Foster, John L., trans. *Love Songs of the New Kingdom*. Austin: University of Texas Press, 1974.

Knappert, Jan, ed. and trans. *A Choice of Flowers: Chaguo la Maua: An Anthology of Swahili Love Poetry*. London: Heinemann, 1972.

———, ed. *Four Centuries of Swahili Verse: A Literary History and Anthology*. London: Heinemann, 1979.

Mayer, Josephine, and Tom Prideaum, eds. *Never to Die: The Egyptians in Their Own Words*. New York: Viking Press, 1938.

Mulford, Wendy, ed., with Helen Kidd, Julia Mishkin, and Sandi Russell. *Love Poems by Women: An Anthology of Poetry from Around the World and Through the Ages*. New York: Fawcett Columbine, 1991.

p'Bitek, Okot. *Horn of My Love*. London: Heinemann, 1974.

Peet, T. Eric. *A Comparative Study of the Literatures of Egypt, Palestine, and Mesopotamia: Egypt's Contribution to the Literature of the Ancient World*. The Schweich Lectures of the British Academy. London: Oxford University Press, 1931.

Stallworthy, Jon, ed. *A Book of Love Poetry*. New York: Oxford University Press, 1974.

Sullivan, Nancy. Introduction to *Love Poems*, selected by Jean Garrigue, xxxv–xxxvii. Garden City, N.Y.: Doubleday, 1975.

Anonymously Written Ancient Egyptian Love Poems

My Love Is Back, Let Me Shout Out the News

My love is back, let me shout out the news!
                My arms swing to embrace her,
And heart pirouettes in its dark chamber
                glad as a fish when night shades the pool.
You are mine, my mistress, mine to eternity,
                mine from the day you first whispered my name!

Translated from the ancient Egyptian by John L. Foster

If I Could Just Be the Washerman

If I could just be the washerman
                doing her laundry for one month only,
I would be faithful to pick up the bundles,
                sturdy to beat clean the heavy linens,
But gentle to touch those finespun things
                lying closest the body I love.
I would rinse with pure water the perfumes
                that linger still in her tunics,
And I'd dry my own flesh with the towels
                she yesterday held to her face.
The touch of her clothes, their textures,
                her softness in them . . .
Thank god for the body,
                its youthful vigor!

Translated from the ancient Egyptian by John L. Foster

I Cannot Condone, My Heart, Your Loving

I cannot condone, my heart, your loving
                 this son of a wild dog who mounted you drunk;
Yet I'll never leave him to judgment, and beating,
                 or wear out my day in recrimination.
Shall I (as they tell me) club him to Syria,
                 cudgel the cur to Nubian exile?
Harry him to the highlands high over me,
                 batter him down to the river mud?
No, not an ear for their harsh clamor!
                 I'll never forswear our swift-running love!

Translated from the ancient Egyptian by John L. Foster

Love, How I'd Love to Slip Down to the Pond

Love, how I'd love to slip down to the pond,
                    bathe with you close by on the bank.
Just for you I'd wear my new Memphis swimsuit,
                    made of sheer linen, fit for a queen—
Come and see how it looks in the water!

Couldn't I coax you to wade in with me?
                    Let the cool creep slowly around us?
Then I'd dive deep down
                    and come up for you dripping,
Let you fill your eyes
                    with the little red fish that I'd catch.

And I'd say, standing there tall in the shallows:
Look at my fish, love,
                    how it lies in my hand,
How my fingers caress it,
                    slip down its sides . . .

But then I'd say softer,
                    eyes bright with your seeing:
                          A gift, love. No words.
                    Come closer and
                    look, it's all me.

Translated from the ancient Egyptian by John L. Foster

Palm Trees, Heavy with Dates

Palm trees, heavy with dates,
        bend over my private garden;
Among such towering friends
        grow tall toward your private dream.
Dear heart, it is I am your chiefest love,
        first bud from the ground of your caring,
And I give back that love, am yours—
        take me and my gift of a garden.
I planted it, weeded it, loved it,
        nursed it to bear this thicket of colors,
Heady with foreign blossoms,
        heavy with all sweet native flowers.
A fountain plays in my garden,
        bubbles below the tall sun,
For dipping your hand in
        while easy we lie
Awaiting the cool of the northern sea-breeze
        that springs upriver at twilight.
A charming spot to stroll,
        your hand covering mine;
My body enjoys, relaxes, plays . . .
        O, how my heart is high
Matching the swing of our going—together,
        halves of a single love!
The sound of your voice is sweet,
        full like the taste of date wine,
And I, drunken girl in a tangle of flowers,
        live only, a captive, to hear it.
But to have you here always, tall in my garden,
        devour you with my hungry eyes—
Love, I'd be raised to pure spirit, translated,
        hovering high over earth!
(See me go! light-hearted! walking on air!)
        Full of such love,

I scorn, insubstantial, the grossness of eating,

        drinking, light-hearted, the bright date wine.

Translated from the ancient Egyptian by John L. Foster

If Ever, My Dear One, I Should Not Be Here

If ever, my dear one, I should not be here,

        where will you offer your heart?

If I cannot hold you close by my side,

        how will you ever know love's satisfaction?

Would your fingers follow the line of my thighs,

        learn the curve of my breasts, and the rest?

It is all here, love,

        quickly uncovered.

Yet would you leave me now

        out of some urge that mankind must eat?

By god is your only organ your belly?

        —are you in love with digestion?

Or is it a matter of dress makes you restless?

        (would you feel naked above me?)

I'm a woman of means—I'll lend you bedclothes!

        Here, hold my breasts to you—

Yours, my offering, full like the love I give

        overflowing, unending . . . (untold) . . .

How splendid a whole day made holy by loving

        (being in touch face to face)—

More than a million times over, my couchmate,

        it shall be heaven,

                good for the soul!

Translated from the ancient Egyptian by John L. Foster

My Love Is One and Only, Without Peer

My love is one and only, without peer,
        lovely above all Egypt's lovely girls.
On the horizon of my seeing,
        see her, rising,
Glistening goddess of the sunrise star
        bright in the forehead of a lucky year.
So there she stands, epitome
        of shining, shedding light,
Her eyebrows, gleaming darkly, marking
        eyes which dance and wander.
Sweet are those lips, which chatter
        (but never a word too much),
And the line of the long neck lovely, dropping
        (since song's notes slide that way)
To young breasts firm in the bouncing light
        which shimmers that blueshadowed sidefall of hair.
And slim are those arms, overtoned with gold,
        those fingers which touch like a brush of lotus.
And (ah) how the curve of her neck slips gently
        by a whisper of waist to god's plenty below.
(Such thighs as hers pass knowledge
        of loveliness known in the old days.)
Dressed in the perfect flesh of woman
        (heart would run captive to such slim arms),
        she ladies it over the earth,
Schooling the neck of each schoolboy male
        to swing on a swivel to see her move.
(He who could hold that body tight
        would know at last
                perfection of delight—
Best of the bully boys,
        first among lovers.)
Look you, all men, at that golden going,
        like Our Lady of Love,

                without peer.

Translated from the ancient Egyptian by John L. Foster

Anonymously Written Ancient Egyptian Love Poems

Flee Him, My Heart—and Hurry

Flee him, my heart—and hurry!—
        for I know all too well this love of yours.
—My antic heart won't let me walk like the others
        but dances off just when I want it home.
It won't wait to let me catch my tunic
        nor stop to let me get my party fan;
It leaves no time to shadow eyes with love lines,
        no time at all to oil my body.

"Don't stand there waiting! Get inside!"
        so heart says when I stand there full of him.
O heart, don't make my aching thoughts turn foolish!
        Why, are we mad? who gave you leave?
                (It's wrong!)
Sit cool, my love, your love comes soon to you.

        But no . . . no, after all . . . there are so many eyes!
These people must not mock me, hissing,
        "You, sister! It's love gone tripping made you fall!"
Hold firm your ground, girl, when you long for him;
        and heart, you shall not flee.

Translated from the ancient Egyptian by John L. Foster

Spell for Causing the Beloved to Follow After

Hear me, O Re, Falcon of Twin Horizons,
                father of gods!
Hear me, you seven Hathors
          who weave fate with a scarlet thread!
O Hear, all you gods of heaven and earth!—

             Grant
That this girl, true child of her mother,
             pursue me with undying passion,
Follow close on my heels
          like a cow seeking pasture,
          like a nursemaid minding her charge,
             like a guardian after his herd!

For if you will not cause her to love me,
        I must surely abandon the day
             consumed to dust in the fire of my burning.

Translated from the ancient Egyptian by John L. Foster

For a Portrait of the Queen

This was a princess.

Of the line royal, lady most praiseworthy
    and a woman of charm, sweet for love,
Yet Mistress ruling two countries,
    the Twin Lands of Sedge and Papyri.

See her, her hands here shaking the sistra
    to bring pleasure to God, her father Amun.
How lovely she moves,
    Her hair bound with fillets,
Songstress with perfect features,
    A beauty in double-plumed headdress,
And first among harim women
    To Horus, Lord of the Palace.

Pleasure is in her lips' motions,
    all that she says, it is done for her gladly,
Her heart is all kindness, her words
    gentle to those upon earth.
One lives just to hear her voice.
    On this wall, by this door, she stands singing,
Great Royal Wife of the Sovereign
    (and a girl King Ramesses loved),
Consort to Power and Majesty
    she is Queen of the Realm, Nafertari.

Translated from the ancient Egyptian by John L. Foster

Traditional Love Songs

Aandonga (Angola and South Africa)

Love Praise

My dark-brown girl is like a cow,
My light-yellow girl is like Nimuene,
As beautiful as Schikuni or Ombago,*
As pretty as a delicately cut thong,
As hides round the loins of a royal servant.
When I wait for her, I can eat nothing,
When I expect her, I cannot sleep,
Sleep and food matter not to me then.
Her fingernails are white as if they were washed,
Her fingers, as if she had just touched fat.
She is as bright as the ombimbo-root,
Ombimbo, dug up by the Bushmen,
Ombimbo, grown in the sandy desert of Amambo,
Picked up at the root of the omusati-tree.
My girl is like a copper ring in looks,
My girl is serious, she does not laugh for nothing,
She does not laugh when we are with people,
She laughs only when we are alone together.
Each time I look into her face
It is as if the sun rose newly.
When I have to leave her
It is as if night came over me.
When she goes for water, help her,
When she treads grain, tread for her too,
When she goes to sow, sow for her too,
When she walks about, carry her!
O my Nehoja, you are my adornment!
All the young men offer you their beads.
My treasure is the most beautiful among all strings of beads,
She is like a delicately cut thong.
Her mother bore her for me.
Since she was born, she has belonged only to me.

I love her dearly even when I am asleep,
But when I am awake, a thousand times more.

* Nimuene, Schikuni, and Ombago are names of cows.

Song of a Bridegroom in Praise of His Bride

Jinkono's Namujezi, Nascheja's grandchild,
Mpingana,* a tree on the plain,
A palm-tree in the possession of Schinkonjo, Nepaka's son,
Belonged to our people of heroes. . . .
Namujezi, you flower from Jinkono's garden,
You plant too high to be reached!
Her noble figure is something to marvel at,
Her beauty turns the heads of the Aalombe,
The people of Jikokola are ravished too.
They run in their eagerness to give Namujezi gifts.
Namujezi's beauty is indescribable.
Jinkono's flower shines like a star.
I saw her from far away, before she came to us.
Namujezi, your eyes—how fresh-new they are!
And your teeth—as if you had gotten them only yesterday!
And your eyes—like those of a hornless cow!
Namujezi, open your eyes, clear as water;
Your teeth—just laugh, laugh out,
So that we may see them all and marvel at them.

We will let our game sleep
Until the morning star appears.
I will not leave the playground so long as Namujezi is there.
Where she is, the moon becomes the sun,
Night becomes bright day.
We are favorites of glorious night,
We are court servants of the moon.
Where you, Star-Namujezi, shine,
I will follow you, no matter where you go.
Well I know the signs of your passing.
Anyone knows Namujezi, even among many women.
She shines like the spring sun rising.
You say: "No one can eat beauty."
Yet I feed on Namujezi's.

* Mpingana is another name of Namujezi's.

Lightning, Strike My Husband

Lightning, strike my husband,
Strike my husband,
Leave my lover;
Ee, leave my lover.
Snake, bite my husband,
Bite my husband,
Leave my lover;
Ee, leave my lover.
    See him walking,
        How beautifully he walks;
    See him dancing,
        How beautifully he dances;
    See him smiling,
        How beautifully he smiles;
    Listen to the tune of his horn,
        How beautifully it sounds;
    Listen to him speaking,
        How beautifully he speaks;
    See him performing the mock fight,
        How beautifully he does it;
    The sight of my lover
        Is most pleasing.
Lightning, strike my husband,
Strike my husband,
Leave my lover;
Ee, leave my lover.

Translated from the Acoli by Okot p'Bitek

Where Has My Love Blown His Horn?

Where has my love blown his horn?
The tune of his horn is well known.
Young men of my clan,
Have you heard the horn of my love?

The long distance has ruined me, oh!
The distance between me and my companion.
Youths of my clan,
Have you heard the horn of my love?

The shortage of cattle has ruined my man!
The poverty of my love!
You men of my clan,
Listen to the horn of my love.

Where has my love blown his horn?
The tune of his horn is well known.
Young men of my clan,
Listen to the horn of my clan.

Translated from the Acoli by Okot p'Bitek

When I See the Beauty on My Beloved's Face

When I see the beauty on my beloved's face,
I throw away the food in my hand;
Oh, sister of the young man, listen;
The beauty on my beloved's face.

Her neck is long, when I see it
I cannot sleep one wink;
Oh, the daughter of my mother-in-law,
Her neck is like the shaft of a spear.

When I touch the tattoos on her back, I die;
Oh, sister of the young man, listen;
The tattoos on my beloved's back.

When I see the gap in my beloved's teeth,
Her teeth are white like dry season simsim;
Oh, daughter of my father-in-law, listen,
The gap in my beloved's teeth.

The daughter of the bull confuses my head;
I have to marry her;
True, sister of the young man, listen;
The suppleness of my beloved's waist.

Translated from the Acoli by Okot p'Bitek

Love Songs

1.

I sleep long and soundly,
Suddenly the door creaks,
Confused, I open my eyes,
And find my love standing there:
What matters death to me?

2.

It has been raining and raining,
It has been raining and raining,
I go out to leave my footprints:
I see the footprints of my love.
All footprints are not alike:
I go out to leave my footprints
And find the footprints of my love.

3.

He has two loves,
He has two loves,
I go to see him off.
I meet the other woman.
I cannot go on,
I cannot go back,
I burst into tears.

Translated from the Akan by J. H. Kwabena Nketia

Love Song

I painted my eyes with black antimony
I girded myself with amulets.

I will satisfy my desire,
you my slender boy.
I walk behind the wall.
I have covered my bosom.
I shall knead colored clay
I shall paint the house of my friend,
O my slender boy.
I shall take my piece of silver
I will buy silk.
I will gird myself with amulets
I will satisfy my desire
the horn of antimony in my hand,
O my slender boy!

Translated from the Bagirmi by H. Gaden

Love Defeats Queen Saran

"Tell Da that I have heard him well,
but I am not alone in this town;
I will call the elders
and let them know of his intentions."

Duga summoned his first son and his advisers
and reported to them Da Monzon's words.
They unanimously concluded
that Da had come to fight,
not to strengthen brotherly relations.

Duga asked for a three days' delay
so that his men who had gone hunting might come back home;
Da Monzon accepted this postponement.

On the day the hunters came back to Kore,

Da was invited to partake of the mead which had been prepared in
    his honor.
Duga's first wife, who had always heard
Da's exploits and good looks highly praised,
was unable to resist the pleasure of seeing him.
Doing so openly was forbidden;
so she came to watch him furtively
through the slits of a millet stem screen.

Duga's wife watched Da Monzon.
She was thunderstruck by his virile splendor;
it was love at first sight and her desire was so intense
that she lost all sense of proper behavior as well as her self-control.
She spent a very bad night, as her flesh
was tormented by a hunger she could not satisfy;

dark thoughts peopled her brain,
she forgot Duga's favors,
she forgot that she was the first queen
of a state famous for the courage of its warriors
and the wealth of its citizens.
She was obsessed by one idea—
to possess Da, to hold him in her arms, to give all of herself to him;
she was lost without knowing it.
Her drunken soul plunged into darkness,
she forgot everything else,
she wanted Da at any price.

She would go mad for him;
for him she would betray
the man who had never denied her anything.
She started thinking about the best way
to confess her love to Da and to convince him
that she was ready to leave everybody and everything
as long as he would belong to her.

She called the seven maids of her household,
her trusted servants, the keepers of her most private secrets,
always ready to sacrifice themselves for her,
and told them, "I am grievously sick,
I will die of this terrible disease."
—"Mistress, how did you, between yesterday and today, catch
so violent a disease that you fear you will die of it?"
—"It entered through my eyes,
then settled in my heart
where it drained the water of serenity
in which my soul was bathing.
My heart is as dry as the balanza tree in the rainy season—
it dries up despite the rains
and turns into white wood, dead wood;
in the same way, in spite of gold and silver, maids and servants,
in spite of a cattle-pen filled with milch-cows,

in spite of granaries crammed with cereals,
in spite of the greatness of my husband,
the fearless hawk that swoops down on the enemy
and picks him up as if he were a chick—woe is me!
I am unhappy in the middle of all these,
and I will die if no remedy is found!"

—"So, what is this strange disease that makes you so miserable,
o! you, good and beautiful mistress?" exclaimed one of the maids.
—"I suffer from a love that burns more than fire,
that pierces more than an arrow,
that cuts more than a razor."
—"You! in love!
You, who, by just jumping over a sick horse,
can cure it of its diarrhea,
you, the precious pearl that only Duga's eyes have seen!
No, mistress, you are trying to mislead us,
you have always loved no-one but Duga
and will never love another."

—"If you do not trust my words
and refuse to help me quench my passion,
then get ready to heat up the water
that will be used to wash my corpse.
If tomorrow at sunrise
I have no hope of possessing the one
who prevented me from sleeping last night,
I swear I will die before the day is over!"

The seven maids opened their eyes wide
and silently looked at each other.
They were wondering whether a bad spirit
had entered their queen's soul
to steal her reserve and her reason
One of them said, "Such is our duty—
we must find a way to cure our mistress

and do everything to save her health."
Kunadi, the oldest of the maids,
told the queen, despite the rule
that forbids to pronounce her name, "Saran,
my good Saran, whom are you in love with?
A genie from King Solomon's palace
or an heir to the throne of the Misra Pharaohs?"

—"No," Saran answered, "the one I am in love with
is neither a genie born of the elements nor a prince from Misra;
he is the son of a Bambara woman,
a stallion that has grown up on the banks of the Dioliba,
he has played under the balanza trees of Segu,
I am in love with Prince Da."

—"Da Monzon! the one who has come to besiege Kore Duga?"
—"The very same. It is stronger than my reason,
it is stronger than my soul,
I am ashamed of it, but I can neither resist nor hide my disease.
This is why I am telling you my deadly secret.
You may choose—either you help me arrange a meeting with Da,
or you denounce me to Kore Duga;
if you prefer the latter solution,
know that Duga will shave my head,
he will cover me with rough tree-barks,
he will load me with vile chains,
just as he has loaded me with gold, silver and precious pearls;
you will see me stumble under whip lashes
before my head is cut off and thrown to the carrion-feeders;
even when my mouth bleeds, my teeth are half-broken and I die
     of thirst,
I will refuse the water that a charitable heart
will offer me to cool down my soul on fire.
I will say, 'Give me Da, it is him I am thirsting for,
water cannot quench my soul!'"

Kunadi looked at her companions—
all were shedding sincere tears,
and Kunadi started crying too.

Knowing that she had deeply moved her servants,
Saran stood up and went into the next room;
she came out with seven snuff-boxes filled with gold
and said, "My beloved maids, I do not know
what tomorrow's sun has in store for me,
so here is a little something for each of you, so that you may live free
in case you are reduced to poverty after my death."
The maids received the snuff-boxes
then withdrew where their mistress could not see them.
They started discussing how to use
the gold Saran had given them unconditionally.
Kunadi declared, "Sisters, being a captive
or a person of low rank
does not exclude having a noble heart;
never has our mistress made us feel
that we are slaves, no better than beasts of burden—
today, by disclosing to us
what may cause her shame and her loss,
and by giving us the means to be free and to live at ease,
she has shown how much she loves us.
So, what shall we do?"
Tenema, the youngest of the maids, suggested,
"Though my years are less than the sum total
of my toes and my fingers,
and though I have neither lived nor seen enough
to tell my elders what to do,
I would like, if you allow me,
to express what my firm conviction is."

"We are listening to you, Tenema, for it may happen
that in a small pond big fish are found
that are never to be found in a lake."

Tenema said, "I think we must stay with our mistress
since we have benefited from her happiness;
we must follow her everywhere and in everything;
let us give her back her gold and let us give her too,
besides our bodies that she already owns,
our hearts, that belong only to us."

Kunadi cast her eyes on her companions;
none looked down,
all looked at her right in the eyes,
their faces beaming with wide smiles
that were in no way faked.
Then Kunadi said, "My sisters,
the youngest among us, that is the one
who has least enjoyed Saran's kind deeds,
has just pointed to us the honorable path.
What do you think?"
As if they were one, the maids answered,
"Let us follow and help our mistress,
may whatever God decides happen,
but let us give her back the gold, let us give her back the gold!"

Immediately, Kunadi gathered the seven snuff-boxes
and went back to Saran with her companions.
She kneeled down in front of the queen and gave her back
her presents that she was holding in a fold of her wrapper.
She said, "Mistress, my sisters and I are bringing back
the gold you have given us to protect
our lives against adversity;
all the gold in the world would not protect us
against the misfortune of being separated from you.
To us you are both life and death.
Everywhere we shall follow you unconditionally,
whether you go through the main gate
or you sneak through the back door;
since God has set a flame in your heart

for Da, we do not have the right
to judge you and even less the right
to try to put out what God has lit.
Tell us what we must do, and we shall do it,
tell us what we must say, and we shall say it."
Saran wept for joy and gratitude.

Saran took out a long roll of cotton strips
and said, "You will help me climb over the town wall.
This very night I will go to Da
and declare my love to him."

The eight women stole away in the dark.
They arrived at the bottom of the wall
in a quiet, seldom watched place.
Saran unfolded the cotton roll
and made a strong and thick rope with it.
She climbed on the shoulders of one of her maids
and heaved herself on the top of the wall;
she then threw one end of the rope to her maids
and took hold of the other;
she let herself slide down the wall
like a bucket that is lowered into a well,
while her maids were counterbalancing her on the other side.
Saran landed with a few scratches,
she shook the rope and her maids pulled it up.
Three of them followed suit
and the remaining four stayed inside
to be on the lookout before the queen returned.

Saran and her companions went up to Da's camp.
A guard saw them and was about to raise the alarm
when he discovered that they were women.
He asked them, "Who are you? Where are you coming from?
Where are you going and what are you looking for?"
Saran walked to the guard and said,

"I will answer but your last question—
I am looking for Da Monzon, go and inform him.
I will wait here with my companions."
Before the sentinel could ask her another question
Saran slipped one of the seven snuff-boxes to him,
saying, "Taste my tobacco,
even though it comes from a woman, you will appreciate it;
I am the one who prepared it, take a pinch and go."
The guard, just by weighing the puff-box,
understood that it contained some metal.
He ran to Da's camp and reported to him.
Da thought for a while. He told himself
that four women in the middle of the night
were a mystery wrapped up in a mystery!
Da jumped to his feet and followed his guard without saying anything
to his advisers who were deeply asleep.
When he reached the place where the four women were waiting for him,
the perfume that filled his nostrils made him understand
that he was dealing with a woman of quality
or, at least, an expert courtesan.

"Good evening, ladies!" Da called cheerfully.
The three maids discreetly stepped backward
and walked away so that Saran and Da
might converse freely.
The guard did the same
and Da remained face to face with Saran.

Saran said, "O! Da! usually it is the suitors
who climb walls to go and offer their hearts
to the lady-loves they sigh for!
This evening, it is the reverse. This is not surprising for there is
no Bambara girl who does not dream of you, o! Da!
All sing your bravery and your dazzling good looks.
All would like to see you, to talk to you, to listen to you.
The other day I could not help hiding

behind a screen in order to listen to you and to have a look at you.
I should never have done so, for then
the devil who has haunted me ever since and cruelly spurs me on
to jump over dangerous obstacles, like the trumpet bird,
would have left me in peace.
But the faintest glimmer of love overcomes
the shadow of convention, however thick it may be.
How many women in love have braved
the darkness of night, rejecting their duty
and dragging their honor in the mud,
to go and find the master of their soul,
the man they would have liked to marry?
I am just another of them,
and I have come, without any shame, to knock at the door of your heart.
Open it, that I may enter it, or have me stabbed
so that, at least, I may die in your arms."

"Who are you, noble daughter of my own race?
Which court have you fled to come to me?"

"I am Saran, Duga's wife."
"You are Saran, Duga's favorite wife, and you . . ."
Da could not go on.

Saran said, "Pleasure for a woman
is not to be adorned with gold and silver,
neither is it to be a monarch's favorite wife,
but it is to live in a simple house
with the man she has chosen.
Such is my case—I am worshipped but unhappy,
I am under constraint but I would like to be free,
free to love the one I love."
Da, realizing that he had, then and there,
a means to learn Duga's most intimate secrets, said,
"Saran, I know you will not accept
to give yourself to me as if you were a courtesan.

We would commit a moral outrage unworthy of us.
But let us be allies, help me;
as soon as I have defeated the so far invincible Duga,
I swear on the spirits of my ancestors
that I will make you the woman you want to be.
So, in front of the whole world, my heart will answer
your heart, that has made me the man you desire.
I shall therefore take you as my spouse,
I shall keep you like a precious treasure
and you will be mine, and mine only."

These words were a solace to the soul and the mind of Saran,
they appeased the heat that propelled her irresistibly forward,
but they fanned in her another fire—
must she betray the man who had married her
against her will, in fact, because she was his subject?
A terrible deal had just been struck
without any witness, between the queen of Kore
and the man who wanted to become its king.
Saran said, "Let us meet again in Kore.
I wish you a good night, o! Da Monzon!"
The two lovers went their separate ways, certain that their secret
was protected by the loneliness of the place
and the deep darkness of the night.

Saran joined her three maids.
She told them, "Let us hurry back to the town before the first cocks
announce the break of day, that revealer of nightly secrets."
The maids perceived in their mistress's voice
the joy she had felt in her heart.
No need to know more, they did not ask any question.
The four women walked back to the wall;
with their hands and their feet, they went back the way they had come.
The girls who were on the lookout were still there, on the alert,
and ready to do everything to cover up their queen's escapade.

Translated from the French by Jacques-Noël Gouat

Women's Song

O handsome Sokoti, O handsome Sokoti, O pretty youth,
Take me and let us go, yes, O master, take me and let us go!
Take me and let us go to the ford across the Agbagnian,
Take me and let us go quietly as far as the ford across the Agbagnian.
O Sokoti, O pretty youth,
O master, take me and let us go, take me and let us go as far as the ford
across the Agbagnian.

I Want to Be with My Love in a Garden

I want to be with my love in a garden
surrounded by pavilions with lovely cushions.
In its center are fountains and water
jetting up like milk.
The nightingale glorifies the orchard
and its seven-colored pears
with songs.

A young man goes from room to room,
gracefully.

The jasmine drops its branches.

Sitting by my friend,
I will be healed.

Translated from the Arabic by Willis Barnstone

I Want to Be in a Garden with My Love

I want to be in a garden with my love,
empty. Not even a gardener.
I want to be in a bath with my love,
empty. Not even a masseur,
and I will bring him all the hot and cold water
he wishes.
Even his sweat I'll collect and put in flasks
so it will make me alive.
The day I am blind from crying,
I will paint my eyes with tears instead of *khol*.

Translated from the Arabic by Willis Barnstone

My Passion Is Like Turbulence at the Head of Waters

My passion is like turbulence at the head
of waters
where boiling rivers sweep away a granite mill.

The sultan of love came to camp in my heart.
I welcomed him
and devised ecstatic nights with him,
but he debated with me and ordered me to satisfy
his every wild quirk.

But he has an untender heart.
I beg him.
He is iron and gives me neither freedom
nor the joy of union.
What causes my pain? Is love a joke?

Translated from the Arabic by Willis Barnstone

Love Songs

I

When I make love with my lover,
it is as if I were cleaning grain
to feed myself: I eat and eat,
a whole field full,
yet my heart is not satisfied.

II

I wish I could put pain in the pans of the scale
To divide it equally between my lover and me.

III

O my dead lover!
As the children put a candle in a lantern,
Light comes through the stones of your tomb.

Translated from the Berber by Willard R. Trask

A Mother to Her First-Born

Speak to me, child of my heart.
Speak to me with your eyes, your round, laughing eyes,
Wet and shining as Lupeyo's bull-calf.

Speak to me, little one,
Clutching my breast with your hand,
So strong and firm for all its littleness.
It will be the hand of a warrior, my son,
A hand that will gladden your father.
See how eagerly it fastens on me:
It thinks already of a spear:
It quivers as at the throwing of a spear.
O son, you will have a warrior's name and be a leader of men.
And your sons, and your sons' sons, will remember you long
    after you have slipped into the darkness.
But I, I shall always remember your hand clutching me so.
I shall recall how you lay in my arms,
And looked at me so, and so,
And how your tiny hands played with my bosom.
And when they name you great warrior, then will my eyes be
    wet with remembering.

And how shall we name you, little warrior?
See, let us play at naming.
It will not be a name of despisal, for you are my first-born.
Not as Nawal's son is named will you be named.
Our gods will be kinder to you than theirs.
Must we call you "Insolence" or "Worthless One"?
Shall you be named, like a child of ill fortune, after the dung
    of cattle?
Our gods need no cheating, my child:
They wish you no ill.

They have washed your body and clothed it with beauty.
They have set a fire in your eyes.
And the little, puckering ridges of your brow—
Are they not the seal of their finger-prints when they
    fashioned you?
They have given you beauty and strength, child of my heart,
And wisdom is already shining in your eyes,
And laughter.

So how shall we name you, little one?
Are you your father's father, or his brother, or yet another?
Whose spirit is it that is in you, little warrior?
Whose spear-hand tightens round my breast?
Who lives in you and quickens to life, like last year's
    melon seed?
Are you silent, then?
But your eyes are thinking, thinking, and glowing like the
    eyes of a leopard in a thicket.
Well, let be.
At the day of naming you will tell us.

O my child, now indeed I am happy.
Now indeed I am a wife—
No more a bride, but a Mother-of-one.
Be splendid and magnificent, child of desire.
Be proud, as I am proud.
Be happy, as I am happy.
Be loved, as now I am loved.
Child, child, child, love I have had from my man.
But now, only now, have I the fullness of love.
Now, only now, am I his wife and the mother of his first-born.
His soul is safe in your keeping, my child, and it was I, I, I,
    who have made you.
Therefore am I loved.
Therefore am I happy.
Therefore am I a wife.
Therefore have I great honor.

You will tend his shrine when he is gone.

With sacrifice and oblation you will recall his name year by year.

He will live in your prayers, my child,

And there will be no more death for him, but everlasting life
     springing from your loins.

You are his shield and spear, his hope and redemption from
     the dead.

Through you he will be reborn, as the saplings in the Spring.

And I, I am the mother of his first-born.

Sleep, child of beauty and courage and fulfillment, sleep.

I am content.

Encouraging a Dancer

Hail, girl
The drums are your drums
May Amma protect your body, your legs
Agile legs, agile arms, come to the drums
Pretty head
All have their eyes on you
You have good milk
All have their eyes on you
You have beautiful sandals
A calabash in your hand
A pretty calabash
All the men have their eyes on you
All the women have their eyes on you
All the children have their eyes on you
All your lovers have their eyes on you
You have beautiful flesh
You have beautiful legs
You have beautiful arms
All of you is beautiful
You have done beautiful things, you have done beautiful
    things, girl, you have done beautiful things
The voice of the drums is in your ears
Come, young men
To the girl, pay over cowries
It is well
She is a beautiful girl

Girls' Secret Love Song

You shake the waist—we shake.
Let us shake the waist—we shake.
You shake the waist—we shake.
I am going to my lover—we shake.
Even if it is raining—we shake—
I am going to my lover—we shake.
I am going to my lover—we shake.
He is at Chesumei—we shake.
Even when night comes—we shake—
I am going to my lover—we shake.
Even if he hits me—we shake—
I am going at night—we shake.
Even if there is a wild animal—we shake—
I am going to my lover—we shake.
A person not knowing a lover—we shake—
Knows nothing at all—we shake.

Translated from the Kipsigi by I. G. Peristiany

Dialogues

I

Man: May I come in, Rasoa-the-well-spoken?
Woman: Come in, honored sir,
I will spread a clean mat for you.
Man: I do not want to sit on a clean mat,
I want a corner of your robe.

II

Man: May I perish, lady!
I passed by your husband's house.
I greeted him, he did not answer;
I asked him the way, he did not speak.
What does it mean?
Woman: Do not be disturbed.
I will keep day and night apart.
The night will be his,
Daylight will be yours.

Girls' Songs

I

Speak to Him-who-receives-fair-praise,
The young Prince to the east of Namehana.
If I call him, I fear people will hear.
If I get up, I fear they will see me.
I wait: tell him my regret.
The skin of him whom I love is perfumed.

II

Tell the clouds to wait,
For the wind is falling.
Tell the lake to forget
For the birds will not come there to sleep.
It is bad to forget all at once,
It is good to forget little by little.

III

I am the child without friends
Who plays alone with the dust,
I am the chick fallen into the ditch:
If it calls, its voice is small,
If it flies, its wings are weak,
If it waits, it fears the wild-cat.
Do not make our love a love of stone
Whose pieces cannot come together;
Make it a love of lips,
Even angry, they draw close and meet.

Love Does Not Know Secrets

Love knows no secrets,
when it is hidden it will be discovered.
Love has no choice;
when it seizes a man,
he will confess everything,
everything that was not done.

Love has no pity,
even an old man may be put to shame,
love does not return
to a Thing it desires.
When it pursues a man,
he turns mad.

Love humbles a man,
his body becomes emaciated;
when a friend of ours is humiliated
it is not fair to laugh at him.
A man does not have the stamina
to put love aside.

Love never agrees
to share a man's attention with
    anything.
If you irritate love,
you melt away at once.
Love is a disease,
a malignant incurable disease.

Love

Love that causes gloom
that is what has crushed me.
Although I am in love
I am badly shaken.
I do not know what to do
to remove this love from my heart.

Love is heavy,
too heavy, it is punishment.
It burns.
There is no doctor for it.
There is no place where one can hide
Love, I surrender.

Where are the joys
that have come to me?
They have all avoided me,
without reason.
Today, love makes me suffer
and punishes me.

My beloved, arrive!
who has such delightful habits,
remove all doubt,
do not change your mind.
I shall be cured
at once, when I see you.

In Praise of Love

Give me a writing board of Indian wood,
ink and a precious pen,
let me praise love for you.

It has entered my heart
forsooth, oh pupil of my eye,
you are like cool antimony.

I will care for you, come to me,
like my eldest child,
your love is not half as strong as mine.

Let me praise love for you
let me tell you what I feel,
so that you can look into my heart.

My heart is full of love,
if it had a lid,
I would open it for you.

For you I would open it,
so that you would know my love,
it is bursting my inmost being.

It is splitting my inside,
and yet I feel no pain,
so much do I love you.

Joy is the fruit of love,
when my purpose is accomplished,
I will give you a present for life.

I will not leave you all my life,
until death may follow,
may we live in mutual affection.

Translated from the Swahili by Jan Knappert

A Match in Petrol

A match, petrol,
when you have put them away,
these are two things
that must not meet,
that could never go right,
the place would certainly explode.
The best thing is to keep them far apart,
then you will have peace.

There can be no peace at all,
that is a certain matter,
fire is sure to break out,
there is not the slightest doubt about it.
Then it will be a problem to put it out,
once the fire has begun to burn.
I have a fire just like hers,
so that damage cannot be avoided.

Do not trust them at all,
not even for one minute,
they do not agree at all,
they will explode at once.
You will expose yourself to danger,
you will be beyond help.
And this thing will be certain:
The fire will not be extinguishable.

Translated from the Swahili by Jan Knappert

To Fatima

Even when she does not look up,
She has a lovely neck;
Even when she is not stretching,
She has beautiful hips;
Her hair is full,
Her neck slender,
Her eyelashes black,
Her eyes white,
Her gums green,
Her teeth bright,
Her belly small,
Her hands soft.

Fatima, the clever one,
When I do not see her,
Bitterness slays my eyes;
When she does not speak,
Bitterness slays my ears.
Because of Fatima, the clever one,
Cold slays me in the evening,
Heat devours me in the morning.
I have filled my heart with words;
So many tears flow out of my eyes
That I scatter holes upon the sand.

To one who is possessed you refuse a cure,
To one who is ill you deny recovery.
Fatima, clever one, say "come,"
And I shall come in haste;
Say "don't come,"
And I shall come anyway.

Translated from the Teda by Johannes Lukas

Complaint of a Jilted Lover

Refuse me if you will, girl.
The grains of maize you eat in your village are human eyes,
The tumblers from which you drink are human skulls,
The manioc roots you eat are human tibia,
The sweet potatoes are human fingers.
Refuse me, if you will, girl.

Translated from the Thonga by Henri A. Junod

Girl's Song

O my cousin, my beloved,
Once I thought I did not love you.
When they came back saying they had left you dead,
I went up on the hill where my tomb will be.
I gathered stones, I buried my heart.
The odor of you that I smell between my breasts
Shoots fire into my bones.

Translated from the Taitok by Willard R. Trask

In Praise of Abazza Ag Mekiia

He who arrived here last night—I think of him constantly.
Mokammed and Salek are like him,
But not like him in charm;
He is smooth with the smoothness of a reed
That stands straight in the water, bright green, and sways;
His white riding-camel kneels, a silver collar around its neck;
Its master—the moon we see there is the substance of which he is made.

by Tekadeit oult Ag-Eklan (b. 1860); Tuareg: Kel Ahaggar

Love Song of a Girl

The far-off mountains hide you from me,
While the nearer ones overhang me.
Would that I had a heavy sledge
To crush the mountains near me.
Would that I had wings like a bird
To fly over those farther away.

Translated from the Xhosa by A. C. Jordan

Zulu Love Song

I saw some maidens, those from the Southland
Who were carrying the pain of lovers
    in their water-jars.
They came to the lake, and poured out the pain.
But back came the Troubler Love, he came
    and he trembled.

Drive me, O Troubler, up to the Northland,
To seek a maiden whose heart is single,
For the heart of these others is double and false!
For the heart of these, I know, is false!

Modern and Contemporary Love Poems

Abderrahim Afarki (Morocco)

A Good Day to You, Si Mohammad

Good morning, Father
you are now settled for good
you are getting used to it, you feel rested
How are things over there?
Most likely, you observe everything we do
our whispers
our laughter
our joy
our sadness
our immense sadness, our so tiny joy
Your care for us
has even increased in your grave
Do you still pray for us?

Flowers are blooming all around you
protecting you
watching over your rest
Droplets of dew
wash your flowers every morning
caress your tombstone
carefully, tenderly
as if they were at your service.
Good morning, Father
the need of you captivates me
your last moments of consciousness captivate me
but my being captivated stifles me
the need of you captivates me
How could you leave when I was not present?
How could you leave without a word of farewell?
Have you forgotten Abderrahman*?

Good afternoon, Si Mohammad
birds land on your tombstone

whisper in your ear
bring you news of the universe
the everyday news you liked so much
tell you about Abderrahman
bring you his love and respect
tell you about his sadness
his deep sadness

Good evening, Si Mohammad
the moon, shy as a mythical bride
smiles at you from high
keeps you company
gets used to your silence
spends her nights as your guest
chases away the darkness that surrounds you
Happy be you
who spends your nights in the company of the moon
your new bride!
You make tea
your strong tea
you fill your glass
and present it to your guest, the moon
your new bride
And your evening starts
punctuated by confidences
She tells you
that Fatima blossoms like a rose
that Zinaba discovers poetry with a child's laughter
that Zahra stares confidently at her future
that Amina is as good as ever
that Saida hides your picture in her heart
that Khadija lives in the rhythm of your memory
that Hassan venerates you in silence
that your wife shyly tells you that she loves you forever
and finds out the burdens of life in your absence
As for Abderrahman

the moon, your new bride, tells you
that she sees him
through the bars of his cell
every night
They meet
gaze at each other
melt in each other

Good night
Father/brother/friend
sleep in joy
in peace
it is getting late
and you are not used to staying
       awake so long

sleep
sleep . . . the moon is watching over you,
       taking care of you
the moon is watching over you, taking care
       of you . . . sleep.

Translated from the French by Jacques-Noël Gouat
* My late father always called me "Abderrahman" (A. Afarki).

The Bad Lover

Leave me, soldier without sense or manners!
I can see that you are full of contempt,
Your hand raised, insults on your lips,
Now that you have had what you want from me.
And you leave, calling me a dog!
Sated with my pleasures,
You'd have me blush for my trade,
But you, were you ashamed
When you pushed gently at my door,
Up like a bull?
Were you coming to play cards?
You turned yourself into something humble,
Agreeing right off to my demands,
To losing all your pay in advance.
And the more your eyes undressed me,
The more your rough desire put you in my power.

When you finally took off my clothes
I could have had your soul for the asking!
I could have cursed your mother
And your father, and their ancestors!
Toward what paradise were you flying?

But now that you've calmed down,
You're back on earth,
Arrogant, rough and coarse as your *djellaba.*

Guest of mine for the moment, my slave,
Don't you feel my disgust and hate?

One of these days
The memory of tonight will bring you back to me

Conquered and submissive again.
You'll leave your pride at the door
And I'll laugh at your glances and your wishes.
But you'll have to pay three times the price next time!
This will be the cost of your insults and pride.

I'll no more notice your clutching
Than the river notices a drop of rain.

Translated from the French by Daniel Halpern and Paula Paley

What Do You Want?

What do you want, girl of the village below?
To marry me, is that what you are thinking?
It is said that you are hardly unfriendly,
and I too dream of holding you.
Here is my only piece of silver.
The peddler will sell you perfumed soap,
a comb, a mirror,—what do I know?
But by my neck, I'll bring you a red scarf
from Demnat if you want.

What do I need, son of the high pasture,
with a piece of silver or silk scarf?

Then tell me what you want—
to marry me? What do you think,
pretty girl of the village below?

You make me laugh, son of the high pasture.
I don't care about money or a scarf,
and even less about marriage.
I expect from you
what you expect from me.
And satisfied, we will leave each other.
What I want, strong son of the high pasture,
what I want is the shelter of this bush
where you will lie on my breasts—which I hold
out to you—and in a moment
happiness sweeter than milk,
while my eyes lose themselves in the sky.

Translated from the French by Daniel Halpern and Paula Paley

Azouou

Azouou! Evening Breeze! What a perfect name!
But why are you so mean?
I won't leave your door
Till it opens,
Or I die waiting.

I see your eyes in the sparking flint.
Your lips against your teeth
Draw me to them.
The peaches of Assermoh have the roundness
Of your breasts,
Your skin has the softness
Of a ring dove's down.
The small blue tattoo between your eyes,
The tattoo on your chin,
The tattoos on your ankles. . . .
And the hidden tattoos—
Will I never see those, Azouou?
Let your hair down over your shoulders.
I will bury my face there
Like a partridge under its wing.

Why do you turn me away?
What do you want?
What gift will please you?

Your voice cuts through my heart
With a sharp edge!
When you walk away
Your hips move within mine . . .

Azouou! Evening Breeze! What holds you back?
Lend me your red lips,
And your moist lips will still be yours.

Lend me your body,
And your satisfied body will be yours still,

And our two hearts will be together.

Translated from the French by Daniel Halpern and Paula Paley

Azouou's Reply

Dear Azou, so well named! Azou!
How could I go on resisting you?
If you see my eyes when a flint sparks,
Can't you see that the powder
Is about to burst into flame?
That I am undoing my hair?
Come in! Close the door and push the lock!
I have ignored your voice long enough.

Why make me sad by talking of gifts
When I want to make you forget my cruelty?
I will give you everything you desire—
My slender tongue and moist lips,
The vise of my crossed legs. . . .

Does it matter that others
Have seen my hidden tattoos?
I sell myself to them.
I give myself to you.
And now you alone exist in my heart.

What are you waiting for?
Undo my belt!
Beloved Azou! Take my lips!
Our mouths will open,
Our bodies will be one
And our two hearts will be together.

Translated from the French by Daniel Halpern and Paula Paley

The Brooch

Grandmother, grandmother,
Since he left I think only of him
And I see him everywhere.
He gave me a fine silver brooch
And when I adjust my *haïk* on my shoulders,
When I hook its flap over my breasts,
When I take it off at night to sleep,
It's not the brooch I see, but him!

My granddaughter, throw away the brooch.
You will forget him and your suffering will be over.

Grandmother, it's over a month since I threw it away,
But it cut deeply into my hand.
I can't take my eyes off the red scar:
When I wash, when I spin, when I drink—
And my thoughts are still of him!

My granddaughter, may Allah heal your pain!
The scar is not on your hand, but in your heart.

Translated from the French by Daniel Halpern and Paula Paley

Love, Love, Love

I opened the closet
That I had closed in my youth.
The love book that I had left
Was covered with dust
The dust that covered it,
I shook it off
The book said: Who is waking me up?
Not knowing it was me.
Even the pages did not recognize me

The book that I had written had forgotten me
As if what it contained
Did not evolve from me
As if another hand had written it
and I was not present
Love that we were ashamed of
All are preaching you today
They beautify you and call you Tayri
To me your name brings me pleasure
How many times have we used it to recall
O my heart the times of my flame
That fire has now died
It has turned into ashes
Carried by the wind it has left me
My youth with it has gone
The traces which remained
Have been covered by the snows of time

The song that could resuscitate it
Does not recognize the sites anymore
Look Tayri what I have become
How much I have changed

But to me the way I have known you
That way your face has remained
Tell me Tayri
You left me at the crossroads
Do you remember when we met
We made the sun shine on our days
The days that betrayed you
Have ended betraying me too
Each has dealt me a blow
Hitting me and missing you

More, more, more

I still talk about you
As if time stood still
Even when I look at your face
I can hardly believe that it is too late
Let me believe in my dream
If you understand me do not blame me
That is all that I have
Times for me will not change

Nothing, nothing, nothing

Nothing is softer than you
And nothing is more bitter
When I believed in you
You held your arms open
You taught me hope
My youth has remained with you
It betrayed both of us
Old age has forbidden your name

Today, today, today

Today, I looked and I saw

Between us a fence of many years
You have not felt the burdens of time
They have fallen only upon me
You know that my friends drink
They have known you before their old days.
They will remain heart-broken

It is over, it is over, it is over

It is over I realize it is too late for me
It is not like the days of my youth
My words are not beautiful anymore
I will burn your book
I will keep your shadow
Only to be reminded of you
It is not under ground
But it is in my heart that I will bury it

Love, love, love

Translated from the Tamazight by Rabah Seffal

It Was Like a Nightmare

It was like a nightmare
When I heard that you had moved
I remained alone with my sorrow
Unresigned to the fact that you were so far away

Should we chance one day to meet again
Please do return my glance
So that among the girls I might still know you
My eyes shall surely remember yours
For you left me badly wounded
Yes, how could I forget you?

And if perchance you should forget me
Just question your heart and it will answer
One day I shall pass by your house
And your heart may remind you of my love
My heart has been broken
And you are the reason for its pain

You were the very first girl
That I ever knew in my life
Indeed you are the key
That opens my heart's desire
But you are also death itself
Since you thwarted my fate

Translated from the Tamazight by Rabah Seffal

Show Me All

I want to feel the hotness of your flesh,
burn in the fire of desire.
I take no pleasure in dreading the unknown;
show me all;
show me the strength of your love
in your full nakedness.

One Kiss

One kiss of parting lovers
which only lasts a moment
will claim
a hundred nights of memories,
a thousand sighs,
as the restless soul searches
in the darkness of solitude,

One swift reunion of lovers
fulfilled in moments
will vanish
a thousand nights of sorrows,
a thousand tears,
as two open hearts
cease to bleed
locked in perfect union
this world forgotten,
as lovers embrace.

Dubem's Patience

The mat I shared with you,
those night visits
that turned
my reluctant legs to lead,
the leaving
quicker than the going.

That was once
upon a time;
you are once
upon a time.

For it is Dubem
with the strong arms,
who gives me yam
from his large store.

It is Dubem,
who says to me,
"Have the children eaten?"

It is Dubem,
who says to me,
"Is your head aching?"

It is Dubem,
who says to me,
"Woman, rest,
I shall finish
the digging for you."

It is Dubem,
who says to me,
"I shall carry
your load for you."

It is Dubem,
who says to me,
"Woman,
the *muli muli*
of your silky skin
outshines
the ripeness
of the red palm-fruit."

It is Dubem,
who says to me,
"Woman,
you keep
the man in me
impatient for the morning light
in which I see
your smiling face."

It is Dubem,
who says to me,
"How I envy
that wet wrapper
that clings
so tightly,
so intimately."

Did our people not say
"It is the patient penis
that eats the bearded meat"?
eeyyeh!
Yes,
it is this patient
Dubem
who will eat
this bearded meat!

A Passing Feeling

Man with misty eyes,
Oh look!
See how the colorful
prairie chicken taps,
vibrates,
in orgasmic rhythms in dance;
the deep oo—oo—oo sound,
like the blowing
of the big cow-horn,
tells its satisfaction
as it dances
for the coming again
of the season of spring.

See how I myself,
in lightness of mood,
leap up into this
bewitching sun-glory
in movements
of loosened limbs,
as I lean forward
my vibrating body
in dance challenges,
right before your moody eyes,
full of worried looks.

Only for this fleeting moment,
join in my own dance,
be a man of the season for now;
be servant
to this compulsive pulsing
of our joyous hearts!

My dance
asks more
than a nodding head.
Yet, it is not forever,
nor is it for worse;

Only a passing feeling,
only a single pleasure,
only this single treasure
of an ecstatic being
of here and now!

Will she deny us
a single pleasure,
the stiff-necked woman,
chained in a golden ring
around her fine finger
in selfish single monopolies!

Gypsy Woman

The short, fat gypsy woman
came rolling to my door one morning,
with sweet-coated tongue and daisies,
eyes shining,
teeth flashing,
she called me a star!
She said it was my special day.

The gypsy woman put wild dreams in me;
a gentle madness of wine
in my head, my mind, my body,
the totality of me,
steady, sure,
head held high,
skirt, black and flowing,
earrings, huge and round,
in ringing echoes of string music,
I stepped onto the pure pavement,
now a terrace of scented gardens,
and crossed the empty street.

Suddenly, there he was!
The world stood still.
Clouds, blue-green
like a rainbowed parasol
came down,
enclosed us, and shut out the world.
Slowly in a daze,
drawing closer
in aromatic dozes of gypsy spell,
we met.

Did I ever see you, my beloved?
I was the slave of a gypsy woman;
I served in bondage for years,

shed so many many tears,
living and wading in dreams,
none heard the silent screams.

You, my beloved, dug in the knife,
till the stars in pain left our heaven;
now a dark forest,
full of stinging rays
from your glittering knife.

One by one, my love,
you killed our daisies,
turning white the gypsy lie.

Alas, today, beloved,
with one last cry,
one last tear-drop,
the blinding clouds recede
and I say, enough!
Surely now,
I am free of the gypsy woman!

The New Warmth

The frosted season of our love
does not end
and the benumbed fingers of our clasped
souls congeal.
We burst into tears of anguish and joy.
Did they say that God shall wipe all tears
from every eye?
I bring my offerings of new corn before your
altar.
Unclasp our hands so I can place them on the
firewood.
In the sameness of the feast we discover the
focal point.
In the bamboo grove of yesterday's desires
And the other day's ambitions
We seek a life in the house of the fire-god
So the benumbed fingers of our souls can
unclasp
And the new fire warm us all.

Lover's Song

There was a time under a bridge
in a foreign country, if I recall,
she came shy weepy.
I told her of love
    and of love's sadness
    solitude and an empty bed.

She answered with silence
dropped a necklace into the grass
turned her head to watch a star.
Then she embraced me kindly
and left a paint in the grass.

Lovers' Song

Call her, call her for me, that girl
That girl with the neck like a desert tree
Call her that she and I will lie in one bed.
When you went away
Isn't it seven years?
Shall I fold mine and say I am cheap
Returned unsold from the market
If they marry a woman don't they sleep with her?
Isn't it seven years now since you went away?

Gabeba Baderoon (South Africa)

Beginning

I turn a corner and see your face.
Our lives spool out from that glance.

I give up everything for this.
I remember everything I've left behind.

You pack your books on the shelves next to mine.
On an envelope addressed to you I write a list of groceries.

You speak to me of your former loves.
You tell me I am your first love.

Before we start the middle of our lives together,
before we contemplate leaving each other,
ceding the subtle map of the bed,

let us linger on a beginning.

Finding You

In your absence I count:
the artist's pencils you grabbed for notes
and your sudden, angled smile
are not here.

My gifts are in one pile, and I do not know
the names on the cards you have received.
My drawings intrigue you, a face
catches your eye.

As I pace this line, I notice
the slow leaking of meanings.
On an envelope addressed to you I
have scribbled a list of groceries.
From the sly beauty of your books
I drink words
like an indiscreet guest;
your thoughts are bookmarks.

Love is shuffling us like cards.

Where Nothing Was

When we met and your face first
clarified itself
from the world,

I tried to find the words
to show where, in my chest,
two senses fired

at once—
touch and sound.
A word for grip and hum together.

A word for the thrum when
the metal chain of an anchor whips
hard and holds.

Or the clout of hands
as trapeze artists grasp each other,
the brief, final clasp

of coming to rest
where you knew
nothing was

a moment before.

The Dream in the Next Body

From the end of the bed, I pull
the sheets back into place.

An old man paints a large sun striped
by clouds of seven blues.
Across the yellow center each
blue is precisely itself and yet,
at the point it meets another,
the eye cannot detect a change.
The air shifts, he says,
and the colors.

When you touched me in a dream,
your skin an hour ago did not end
where it joined mine. My body continued
the movement of yours. Something flowed
between us like birds in a flock.

In a solitude larger than our two bodies
the hardening light parted us again

but under the covering the impress
of our bodies is a single, warm hollow.

Juma Bhalo (Kenya)

The Eyes or the Heart?

1

I bring accusations   let them reach every place
what has happened to me   let me explain it all
I, your friend, am grieved   I am not satisfied even when I eat
from thinking of the misfortune   that has happened to me.

2

I blamed myself   I put the fault on my heart
for making me infatuated   while I loved the beloved
it came about that I had no time   even to want to sleep
because of the many anxieties   and the difficulty I found.

3

So I took my heart to judge it   "Why give me this low
    state of mind?"
and it answered, "Understand   I, your heart, am not at fault
you had better blame   what saw the beloved
they were the first to see   and to give me the desire."

4

And when I went back to my eyes   to show them their fault
they also defended themselves   "It is the heart that brings
    unhappiness
our job is just to look   we don't eat a thing
the heart loves the beloved   this is slander for us eyes."

5

And my heart answered me   "Well, then, say, what next!
this is useless, don't trouble yourself   looking for the one at fault
it is the eyes, it is because of them   that I like the place
because they are the ones who saw   and so I desired."

6

On going back to my eyes   they would not accept responsibility
and they swore an oath to God   showing that they were not at fault
and when I went back to my heart   it said, "Never, never in your
    life
blame the one who saw   for it was then I began to desire."

7

My friends, these things astonish me   these two things together
you will bring judgment   show me the one at fault
that I may know what to do   which one made me unhappy
either my eyes by seeing   or should I blame my heart?

8

The end, I finish it   where it has stopped, O messenger
when He comes who is the Judge   to show me the one at fault
let him not make unlawful judgment   let him judge rightly
so that I may know the one with troubles   either the eyes or
    the heart.

Translated from the Swahili by Lyndon Harries

The Love of Which I Speak

The love of which I speak,
so that we may all enjoy it one day,
is praising one another's hearts,
then we shall be one.

That is the best love
for wise people;
they will receive every treasure,
when their intentions are pure.

The profit of loving one another
has no equal;
nor have I seen anything like it
in this world.

When mortals love one another
they will live in mutual understanding forever;
and many things will succeed,
with purity of intention.

Those who possess true love
in their hearts
will protect one another against suffering,
and will show each other the way.

Love, that is the origin
of people being together,
and if that were not so,
evil would have no end.

Love is a necessity,
that is the beginning of unity;
it brings people together in society
so they become one.

Love, even in religion,
God the Giver has commanded us
that we must love one another,
that we must not treat each other badly.

Love is a wall
which will stop war;
they will not persist in discord
who love consciously.

Love is peace
and mercy on earth;
that is a priceless thing,
it means we are all together.

A Certain Person

1

In the beginning   I begin by asking forgiveness
I do not want you to blame me   with your tongue
love is a poison   the loved one does not see
   though she be shown visibly.

2

The wound   which I have inside me
pierces my heart   and cuts me to the heart
because of my love   for a certain person
   where I go I have no peace.

3

I find difficulty   because of the longing which is in my heart
it increases a thousandfold   all day long I speak of her
on the path I am like a blind man   now I see, now I do not
   for thinking of a certain person.

4

I swear   by God
it is by God's Name   that I swear to Him
my heart is troubled   because of love
   show me the way that I may go forward.

Translated from the Swahili by Lyndon Harries

My Beloved

1

I bring you greetings   my beloved, respond
read well and understand   everything I have written
in my disconsolate state   because love has hold of me
and do not blame me   my heart wants you.

2

It is not I who want disgrace   I want what is right
it is my heart which prompts me   to proclaim these things
towards you it suffers pain   it does not act normally
please satisfy me   give my heart what it wants.

3

It hurts me so much   concerning you my heart gives anguish
so that it has no choice   it spins round like a top
whether night or day   if you are mentioned it is startled
please hide me   lest I be destroyed.

4

I give you my most inmost thoughts   believe in the Lord God
when I see you, my love   my heart is split apart
and my eyes see nothing   my legs shake
and then when I am asleep   if I dream of you I start up.

5

And what drew me   to your dear self, just listen
is your eyes and your eyebrows   especially when you laugh
and then your diction as well   and the shape you were made
when I look at you I never stop   I get confused for sure.

6

There are many things that trouble me   nor shall I write them all
but the thing that eats me up   and makes my blood dry up
is what I am telling you   so don't say it is a joke
this is what eats my heart out   and makes me lose my senses.

7

The writer has written   listen to my desire, listen
Don't be angry with me   and grow resentful
You can answer me   "I do not want" or "I want"
so don't find it difficult   according to your liking, speak.

Translated from the Swahili by Lyndon Harries

Syl Cheney-Coker (Sierra Leone)

To My Wife Dying of Cancer (1)

For Dalisay

To see you lying on the couch propped up with pillows,
     drinking those sour juices of wheat grass , apricot kernels,
and silkworm milk, blended to halt the hand
of this odious sentence, was not the worst knife of all,
but to remember the summers when you did not need to knit
     colourful Afghans to bring out the sunflowers in your eyes.

Nothing prepares us for the un-symmetry of God: this cruel hand,
     when, even after the Pelvic Exoneration, you were uncomplaining,
deprived of much that is woman from the chemo that sapped you
like a reluctant banana transplanted from the tropics to Antarctic.

You sat up to watch the TV, constant companion in your agony,
but never gave up the habit of reading:
a raccoon digging for knowledge in a forest;

     Dreaming of home, we used to walk by the lake in Guymon,
     feeding the squirrels, mocking the squawking geese,
     and listening to Chris, the old man next to our apartment,
complained about his legs, but at least he was able to drive.

 Now, it is you that lie waiting for a new God all day long,
 as I sit holding your hand , flying in from Las Vegas,
even though the tarantulas of security and agonies
 of wait at the airports are scripts undeserving of memory.

After twenty four years of a love begun in Manila,
and tested in the desert of Maiduguri, then Freetown,
your wish was to live long enough to return
     to the river flowing in front of the house in Juba:
     my last book of the trilogy that you insisted I must edit.

In the expectation of miracle, Malaika and Davey
pray for a word from God, and I marvel at the strength
that keeps you going without bitterness, this side of tragedy.

To My Wife Dying of Cancer (2)

Last month, I moved you into the hospice,
after those chemo journeys to hospitals
and clinics smelling of painful prognosis, sharp as raw pepper.
Restrained as statuettes, the doctors said their goodbye.

    Seeing you reduced to dependency, this pain
      that does not respond to cure, your hallucinations
      come in English and Tagalog like a tormented juxtaposition.
Like a conductor's slow movements, you move your arms
 to an orchestra of mute players, ready with bone harps and limpid
drums.
 And I go on thinking that life is not a river's rhythm,
 not a lark's sweet violin ascending to the sky;
 for even when you couldn't see the sun , you had a smile
 to make the weeping willows bloom outside of your window.

    The feel of autumn turns the leaves yellow.
Rain is falling: sweet memory of my tropical youth,
now that my life is so near to being tragic.
But, dear God, that woman lying inside,
    who is all bones: a reduced narrative of skeletons;
who will not see the leaves changing their colours.

    Bring her quickly to your sunny world,
for the song that would keep her alive and smiling
died a long time ago in the flute of your lips that are silent.

Homecoming

I come home with the ashes of she who was my wife,
my Polaroid eyes falling on the empty rooms
where she will no longer walk. Fragile as flower,
my mother comes from her own grave to console me.
In the study, I do not even find a pen; the desk on which
I write this poem eaten away by termites.

No dogs play in the yard, I think of their old brawls—
the bullet-riddled one, especially, that I buried
near the spot where my wife planted the avocado:
its crude stump now yawning a dwarf in my heart!

Having buried so many of them,
        the dead deserve a quiet place in my garden,
but I speak angrily of one disagreeable man,
who destroyed the avocado; all the other trees
in my yard hacked—his ghost a ghoulish presence
in his unfinished house; the nights of his noisy relatives
his legacy of a wanton dream to torment me,
as I go to sleep, thinking of planting a new tree
for a soul that was always smiling.

Poem for a Lost Lover

to Merle Alexander

Eyes of heavenly essence, O breasts of the purity of breasts
Russian sapphire of the blue of eyes
O wine that mellows like the plenitude of Bach
Sargassian sea that is the calm of your heart
the patience of you loving my fragile soul
the courage of you molding my moody words
I love you woman gentle in my memory!

O woman of the thirst of Siddhartha's love
you that I lost in the opium of my youth
have you fallen among the rocks off the New England coast
or now in premature grey nurse a stubborn tear
at the window watching winter's snow-coated leaves
here the tropical blossom of an African November
breathes gently on the tree of my heart
Oh that you could have known it woman of the sexual waters
heart of the spirit born of that love
dressing continents with garlands for whom I say
night strike my heart with the purest verse!

Frank M. Chipasula (Malawi)

Chipo::Gift

for Helen

Another gift from home searches nine months
for the underground route I took out,
years wriggling out of the man-made crocodile
on Mponda's copper-beach shore,
your firm arms splitting the beast's jaw. You,

mysterious Alice we misnamed Gift,
swam through my blood into your mother's blood,
till, beached on the sweet island, you basked awhile;
Then, daughter with divine and noble feather,

You carried your baskets brimming light,
crossed wild oceans, past lavish mansions,
and chose our humble nest to grow your wings.

Hands That Give

for Pat

Are open doors; they bear the cross of the rose;
Are petals of love to the famished mouth.
Wheat was made for your arms thick to the
       elbow in dough—
In your hands everything turns to prayer:
Love ripples through it; life pulses through it.
Hosannas rise highest from your fingers
       to my ravenous mouth.
(Mothering, you have mothered me
       through the times that thrust their lean
bodies into my helpless arms.)
The dough and our children awaken
       from our breath from our heartbeats;
Like my silent aunt you roll your breath
       in the sweet bread dough—
Out of poverty you knead a new loaf
       to feed the gods in us.
A cake, a loaf of surprises and bread rolls
roll out from the flour, love and tears;
butter milk, drops of sobs and sweat.
Into all this you dissolve your self.
From these hands I replenish my self.

Once, when I fell from the twentieth century,
Your hands polished my soul till it glittered.
Besides my ribs, two soft hands lassoed
to clean attentive ears, like fluffy rabbits,
raked my back, peeled the pain from my mind,
and shortened the lean legs of exile.

Out of the oppressive fumes of the kitchen,
These hands release a feast from your magic horn
Onto the altar of our secret shrine.
In the heart of each cake you conceal a crystal star.

The Kiss

after Rodin, after Bloom

This marble kiss will never erode, never fade,
From the stone lips sealed with sweetness.
The rock's fine fingers are wings on her marble skin;
The birds of his palms are flying over her,
Softly sifting love onto her bared thigh.
His body, kissing hers, suddenly surges awake:
Music burns through his veins, every cell sings.
In his arms flow a million gallons of blood
That flowed through the arms of generations.

Her lips, having carefully read his body,
Rest on his own, read the Braille of his lips,
Her palm fronds fan the fire.
As they dance up the ancient fig tree,
His fingers fanning the flame he kindled in her loins,
Oils welling from her secret river anoint him,
Coating him as he stirs her soul in the flesh bowl
Where their lives blend and thicken forever—

At both ends where they are neatly joined
He is pouring his turbulent life into her—
Their tongues stirring storms in their mouths.

As she laves him with her own,
His needle dances in the grooves of her song,
Their tongues licking songs inside their mouths:
The double kiss doubles their joy.

Wife/Life

Pat

My friend, my sister, my wife,
rhyme weaves you into my life.
Now the two letters shuttle me
between you and life, wife
of my youth and now my midlife,
between nature and nurture, what was
Eve and Adam, the garden you carry
and a brook that, sleeping, awakes to my thirst.

Between us we reseal our dreams with kisses,
your lips on my heart
beat, on my pulsing sweet root,
your hands kneading the sweet dough
into a hard-baked breadstick
that enrages your hunger.

I cannot drop you without breaking my life.

For my hunger you offer brown loaves
and a chalice of consecrated honey for my thirsty
root through which my sacred spring
surges towards your buried honey
that rages like a sacred volcano
your fiery thighs, twin songs that braid my back
your arms, vines that bind me to this house
whose shoulders prop up my pain-drenched body.

In you, my mother, your mother
and the mother of my children,
is my wife and my life:

Wife, you *are* my life.

A Song in Spring

for Masauko

My son dances in the circle
of his own light:
See his feet blossom
as he dances to a distant song.

My son dances, steps over the sun:
He has caught the sun in his palm!
He rubs the sun with his fingers
His fingers bloom, his fingers are

The sun that he caught, are the flower
That he waves as he dances in the circle

Of his own light
Of his own sun.

Siriman Cissoko (Mali)

O Tulip, Tulip I Have Chosen

I

O tulip, tulip I have chosen from among all the flowers of our
    great races of men!
I sing your slim black body, I tell of your slender girl's body,
    of your suddenly flashing eyes
I cry aloud the blue palm tree of your lashes
The broadswords of your plaited tresses, commas of lightning
    stabbing the sky.
I shout your charms, ah! your lips that are fleshy dates!

II

Young woman, full bosomed, loins more fertile than the banks
    of the Nile
I will wait for you when in my vast orchards the mangoes like
    censers breathe out their smells;
And the wind sways the great fans and most delicate gifts.
Then, on an evening of *bairam*, very early you will come,
    O beauty of blackness, under your white veil.
I will welcome you among wedding songs and rhapsodies of
    blood.
I will be clothed all in dream, but no mirror in my hut
Only the green of your eyes where I may drown my longing.
I will gird me with the strength of the young men to carry you
    off more swiftly leaving the impatient matrons without.
Woi! You will be my glory, I your pride, O Beauty of blackness!

III

Sope, when you are gay, when you are gay, Sope
Your smile caresses my eyes.

Then I would become your joy, to unfold your tulip face.
Yes, die upon your lips, quench myself in your voice,
Yes, drown in your dark eyes.

When my dark lady walks, the desire takes me to be under her
     feet.
That I might kiss her feet, that they might trample my heart,
     ah! Lord!

When my dark lady adorns herself, she is Sogolon, the Malinke
     Princess.
Would I were boubou, jewels, golden slippers.

Between my fingers, from thread and from gold and from leather
Let me weave her body in finest diamonds, in my glittering
     poems.

José Craveirinha (Mozambique)

Just

Love,
Not so much
Please

Now and again
take me in your arms
and wrap me in the brown and yellow caress of your desire

Now and again
so that I can forget
until morning when they come to get us
and we don't know if we'll be back
and if we're man or thing
and if we can know the nature of true laughter
and if this be true or false
Call the Children
and the house
and the woman with the frightened eyes
without the waking appearance of remorse

Love,
not so much
please

Just now and again

take me in your crossed arms
and wrap me in the brown and yellow caress of your love
and in the peaceful certainty of your affection

Now and again

Just now and again
take me in your arms
my love

Translated from the Portuguese by Arthur Brakel

David Diop (Senegal)

Rama Kam

song for a black woman

I like your wild beast look
And your mouth that tastes of mango
    Rama Kam
Your body is black spice
That makes desire sing
    Rama Kam
When you pass
The loveliest girl envies
The warm rhythm of your hips
    Rama Kam
When you dance
The tomtom Rama Kam
The tomtom stretched like a victorious sex
Gasps under the drummer's leaping fingers
And when you love
When you love Rama Kam
A tornado quivers
In the lightning night of your flesh
And leaves me full of the breath of you
    O Rama Kam!

Close to You

Close to you I have regained my name
My name long hidden beneath the salt of distances
I have regained eyes no longer veiled by fevers
And your laughter like a flame making holes in the dark
Has given Africa back to me beyond the snows of yesterday
Ten years my love
And mornings of illusion and wreckage of ideas
And sleep peopled with alcohol
Ten years and the breath of the world has poured its
    pain upon me
Pain that loads the present with the flavor of tomorrows
And makes of love an immeasurable river
Close to you I have regained the memory of my blood
And necklaces of laughter around the days
Days that sparkle with joys renewed.

To My Mother

When memories rise around me
Memories of anxious halts on the edge of the abyss
Of icy seas where harvests drown
When days of drifting live in me again
Days in rags with a narcotic flavor
When behind closed shutters
The word turns aristocrat to embrace the void
Then mother I think of you
Your beautiful eyelids scorched by the years
Your smile on my hospital nights
Your smile that spoke old vanquished miseries
O mother mine and mother of all
Of the negro who was blinded and sees the flowers
    again
Listen listen to the voice
This is the cry shot through with violence
This is the song whose only guide is love.

Isobel Dixon (South Africa)

Love Is a Shadow

she-camel bucks the wind,
curls back her supple lip
at her own scent

she has not stored enough
for drought like this
is thirsty, thirsty

going down to Egypt
with her clumsy, rolling gait
snorting, crying after shadows

in the changeless desert
after sandy crescent moons
where horses' hooves

have galloped, gone away

Aftertaste

The vineyard's moonlit coolness
slipped around us, soft chiffon,
as I held out to you sweet hanepoot
knowing deeply how your lips
would brush upon my fingers as you bit
the firm flesh from the stalk.

Now so cultured, as you stand and talk
you sip unconsciously
your hand curled carelessly about the stem—
a rather special year our hostess said—
its subtle bite upon my tongue
too chill and rather dry.

You, Me and the Orang-utan

Forgive me, it was not my plan
to fall in love like this. You are the best of men,
but he is something else. A king
among the puny; gentle, nurturing.

Walking without you through the zoo, I felt his gaze,
love at first sight, yes, but through the bars, alas.
Believe me, though, it's not a question of his size—
what did it for me were his supple lips, those melancholy eyes,

that noble, furrowed brow. His heart, so filled with care
for every species. And his own, so threatened, rare—
how could I not respond, there are so few like him these days?
Don't try to ape him or dissuade me, darling, please.

For now I think of little else, although
it's hopeless and it can't go on, I know—
I lie here, burning, on our bed, and think of Borneo.

Cusp of Venus

We lay together, hot, but innocent,
the lawn our green-sprung bed
inside the warm tent of the darkness,
blanketed by stars.

Then, touching, touching, whispering
for hours, sometimes you shielded me
from bats or comets, or the night breeze
creeping up on us.

As heat and gravity pressed you to me,
I knew that I would always be here—
in your orbit, moist, aglow—
while stars spilled past

down to the far side of the world,
to other nights and other budding lovers
learning how to topple heaven and earth.

Intimacy

She tried not to wake him, weeping
with his arm still cast across her,
a man in his deep and sudden sleep.

Such dammings up. Was it the heave,
despite herself, of her breast,
or the hot salt sliding to his skin

that made him reach out blindly
for her face: wiping each cheek
with large and tender hands,

though she knew from his breathing
and the morning's bright, clean slate,
that he was only dreaming, half-awake.

Giving Blood

You did it once. They strapped
the velcroed pad around your arm
and your veins grew,
blue and luminous and huge.
Your heart pumped fiercely,
with enormous thuds
and the blood gushed,
thick red splattering the bag.
Watching the flood and smash of it
you felt the needle jumping
wildly in your vein
and even after hot, sweet tea,
a biscuit, rest, the room whirled,
darkened when you stood.

Crude biology alone attests
to your impatient energy:
I listen to the anecdote and know
you are too fast, too furious for me.
I'm pale and slow; my head spins easily.
They've sent me home before,
my heart too cautious, pressure low,
no good. So I'm glad that something—
needle breaching skin—can frighten you,
but still feel a stab, my weakness,
grudging awe. And if I'm honest, more:

a fierce, hot flush suffuses me.
I am drawn, repulsed, humiliated, drenched.

Emanuel Dongala (Congo Republic)

Fantasy under the Moon

(Blues for a muted trumpet)

I climbed towards you on a ray of moonlight
that filtered through a hole in my straw-thatched house
When I had reached the smiling arch of your mouth among the
    stars
you came to me
open under the sea of your body the heaving wave under my body
my heart beating to the rhythm of yours moving to the rhythm of
    your tribe the people of the mountain;
your serpent form writhing beneath mine
I sucked your cobra's poison from your broken lips
and my fever mounted like a sickness.

I visited last night our banana grove of the first time.
When I reached those great somber aisles
under which we pressed each other behind your mother's back
under the teasing trumpet of thirsty mosquitoes
the circle of my arms about your shadow your phantom
all at once hung emptier than the rope of a wine-tapper
embracing the palm tree.

I don't know why that large cloud crossing the moon
suddenly made the tide of your body fall.
Like oiled wrestlers at a festival
who feel their adversary slide between their arms
powerless I felt you slip from mine
under the moon's light white as this wine as your teeth which made
    you so gay
as you fluttered wildly in the circle of the dance
while your mother warned you not to come near me.

I looked up at the sky from the depths of my hut;
the moon was only a smile, your white smile congealed.

Love in the Daytime

My lover
Shines like the sun.
I may be burned
Black as a frying pan,
Sweating buckets
And keeling over
With vertigo,
But why worry?

My lover
Shines like the sun.
She pours over my body
And breathes into my soul.
It feels so good
When she lights
My love on fire
Like dry wood.

Translated from Tigrinya by Charles Cantalupo

"I Love You" II

Young and afraid
I should have said
"I love you."

I hear her reply:
"You really want me? Ssshh.
Send your father to mine."

Shy, greener than green,
I couldn't say it.
"I love you."

Translated from Tigrinya by Charles Cantalupo

Ferenji and Habesha

Hey sugar.
Hey shkor.
Come 'ere honey.
I love you, mAr.
Oooh, my sweetest.
You're the best.
I'm crispy little bread.
I'm hard thick crust.
Have some honey wine.
Taste this dark sorghum beer.
Do we need a car?
Nah, a mule suits us fine.
Let's build a home.
We'll make it like our poem.
Near the city for fun.
But far enough away to relax in.
Hey Habbash. What you want Ferenji?
Kiss me. Not in public, sweet ass.

Translated from Tigrinya by Charles Cantalupo

Whose Daughter?

If I can't have her
Every morning every day
My head aches.

I take her at breakfast
And after breakfast.
I want her at lunch
And after lunch.
I need her at dinner
And after dinner.

She slides through my lips
And licks my tongue.
She comes in my mouth
And I'm a man
Down to my core.

Burning incense,
I take her leisurely
On my sheepskin at home.
If I need her really bad,
Any bar we're in will do,
And I take her standing up.

Whose daughter would do this,
Kiss after kiss after kiss
All day and all night long?
Is such behavior wrong?
Look in your pot on the fire.

I'll tell you her name—coffee.

Translated from Tigrinya by Charles Cantalupo

Talking about Love

Talking about love
Depends . . .
Is it hot or cold?

Talking about love
Doesn't end.
Is it sour or sweet?

Talking about love,
Don't pretend.
The human heart

Gave birth to love
And an identical twin—
Hate—

Stalking us to this day.
Talking about love
We deal with both.

Translated from Tigrinya by Charles Cantalupo

Silas

Silence so deep
It can be heard,
And a full moon—
A peaceful night,

Until a bird
Starts whispering,
Chirp, chirp, chirp.
He wants his mate

And over there
Right away
Another bird
Loud and clear

Replies, *I'm here*
For you, my hero.

Silas, listen.
Please don't be dense.

What the bird says
Is *yes* to love.
Silas, say *yes.*
Love's calling you.

Enough silence.
Answer *yes.*
If you give, you get,
And then we rock.

Silas, listen.
Please don't be dense.

Translated from Tigrinya by Charles Cantalupo and Ghirmai Negash

Let's Divorce and Get Married Again

I worried about you
Having your first child,
But rising like the star
The wise men saw
You overcome my fear
And I bowed to your light.

It felt like an earthquake
As thunder filled the sky
And the seas seemed to part.
My world went wild,
Making my poetry soar
In the ululation
Of your opening life's door.

Not long after the birth
And christening, did someone make
You change, threatening
And pushing me away?
Could anyone give you more
Of his heart than me,
And giving it all for your sake?

So now what can I say?
If I whispered
In your ear, "Let's divorce
And get married again,"
Would you feel better,
Like you did back then?

Translated from Tigrinya by Charles Cantalupo and Ghirmai Negash

Naana Banyiwa Horne (Ghana)

Sounding Drum

There is a universe buried inside of me.
A hibernating hide
waits
anxiously
to be sounded.
Sounded by the vibration that is you.

The inside of me is a sounding drum.
A pulsating drum,
suspended,
pulsing,
toned,
by the tenderness that is you.

I am a universe.
A drum sounded into life by the rhythm
that is you.
Your heart drums me into sound.
Your heart beats my drum,
my song.

At last!
The drum that is me
vibrates with rhythm
that is you.

You Rock My World

You rock my world,
man of primeval passions.
Your rousing touch ignites
every atom in my care-ridden body.

Miracle maker
injecting life blood into me,
I cherish your invitations
to the threshing floor of healing.

For always I emerge, purged of all tension,
resonant in rhythms that are vibrantly radiant.
Your manhood draws out my womanhood.
Your touch lifts me high above life's drudgery.

My maker must have given you the key
to my sanctuary.
For you have unlocked the door
to the secret of my life.

Miracle maker
Your touch unleashes
that primal joy of knowing
how well loved I am.

Sore Ka Pra: *Whoopie, Akan Time*

Before alarm clocks,
Akans had *Sore ka pra.*
Sore ka pra of tender genesis.
Rousing feather strokes, energizing drowsy wives.
Husbands passionately beget happy homemaking.

Sore ka pra!
"Wake up and go sweep" erupts into
husband passions pestling tender
offerings into enraptured mortars.
Wives bask sensuously in
the tender embrace of husbands.
The rhythm of pestles encircled
by the syncopation of mortars.

Sore ka pra!
Cherished secret of women breezing through
their day's chores.
Fully-sated, wives spill marital contentment,
creating anew a slumbering world
in intricately executed broomstrokes.
Signatures!
Signifiers
of marital bliss.

Happy Father's Day

June 20, 1992

I wake up with you on my mind.
Man of my life,
begetter of my children.
I wake breathing,
tasting,
feeling,
smelling,
seeing you.
Not in my mind's eye, but in my being.
Sewn as you are inside the fabric of my being.

So I console myself I can stand
this physical separation imposed
by the necessity of our lives
and all the lives that tie into ours.
I leave you with all I love
and set out, the proverbial heroine.
I go to slay the dragon that dogs our lives.

I come back wiser than I left maybe,
but certainly bearing fruit—the stock
of that harvest we sowed together
at the beginning of our becoming.
On this father's day away from you,
I hail you father-mother-companion.
Progenitor of me and ours,
I cannot find enough ways to serenade you.
Oyeadze!
Me da wo fom.

Ahmad Basheikh Husein (Kenya)

Messenger, I Send You

Messenger, I send you, if you are intelligent,
go quickly and ask, that I may know,
does love hurt, or is that lies and slander?

Noble gentlemen, civilized and cultured,
I want information, I seek your reply,
is love a quality, or is it a disgrace?

Furthermore, ask them, the readers of law,
to tell you the truth, not to deceive you,
is love permitted, or is it prohibited?

Furthermore, explain these words to the physicians;
remember well what I am telling you,
is love a disease, or is it a state of health?

Also to the medicine men do not omit to go,
confess your ignorance, so that you may learn,
is love a being tied, or is it to act?

And those with understanding, all the worldly people,
even madmen, argue my point with them,
is loving sweet, or is it bitterness?

And those without intelligence, with blind hearts,
ask them this without circumlocution,
is love truth, or is it a lie?

Youngsters, children, even imbeciles,
and interpreters of dreams, repeat (the question) to
    them all,
is love hot, or is it cold?

Even the animals, go to them and try them,
and if one is not sure, ask his fellow,
is love inside, or is it outside?

Even the inanimate beings, even those that cannot hear,
and sky and earth, ask them all,
is love good fortune, or is it being unlucky, unhappy?

Accept knowledge, so that you may know what to say,
go and ask death, the great mourner,
is loving dying, or is it salvation?

Get up, hurry, quickly, let them give you the answer,
that I may finish worrying,
is love black, or is it white?

Love Is Not Sweet

The scholars of Syria and all those from Hejaz
have already given their opinion in clear words;
love is not sweet in these times.

Wiles and cunning tricks are now very frequent,
and good words are no longer heard;
love between two people is lacking.

When you behave honestly towards her, my friend and
     comrade,
she will reply with anger and abuse;
unrequited love, what pleasure is
     there in it?

Even if you ran all the way, you would not be able to
keep up with it,
and when you give her this person, she does not even
say thank you;
the one who follows his heart will regret it afterwards.

My brother, accept the words I have spoken;
even if you give your money, of all kinds;
love between two people is lacking.

I Have No More to Say: Love Is Finished

What is that important thing you want to show me?
There are many words, which remain to be verified;
I have no more to say—love is finished!

This is not the way to please a heart;
people are talking about you, because of what you did;
how can you eat together with your husband?

Do not make light of it, the way you have been treated;
because your condition is not what it once was;
that surely is the evidence that you have been turned
    down.

If it had not been for eating together,
you would be killing yourself for nothing, for someone
    who does not want you;
this being turned down is not the same as being told
    to get out.

I warned you, stop your cunning,
you please me only when you do no evil;
you are playing with abundance, you will suffer poverty.

Do you not understand this, or is it on purpose,
to be bled white without useful purpose;
a useless thing does not last long; you could have been
    useful to yourself.

Deeds are sufficient for a man to understand;
it is better to stay away and make yourself scarce;
if you delay, you will be poisoned.

Handle your love affairs carefully, do not cause irritation,
once the heart has turned away, it will not return.
I am capable of love, but I can refuse it too.

Let us make a riddle, let us give it a description,
let us speak of many things and let the people hear it
    clearly;
he who does not fear a bull, must be himself a bull!

He that never strikes it lucky, will not be appreciated;
to be luckless is disaster, it is to be caught sinning;
where there are trees, there are no builders: luckless is
    the land untended.

No one gets wishes to whom they are not allotted;
you may pretend pride, but you are only giving yourself
    trouble;
love is a question of luck and predestination.

There is an end to all actions,
my heart, be not deceived, you would have to bow down
    later;
that is what one has to do in time, to see through the
    wicked world.

You are suffering in vain, but I am not prepared to go,
nor even to intend it, nor indeed did I act,
do not think that all is easy, much has to be built.

Great regrets, I feel sorry for what I miss,
I cultivated a field—of withering trees,
I planted good plants, I am reaping rotten things.

Rashidah Ismaili (Benin/Nigeria)

Clandestine

Circuitous, ambulatory,
my feet trace darkened streets.
Spurred on by an insatiable need
to be fulfilled, I go down and
around a new place with strange names.

Hugging brick walls I move
wrapped in a full length cape.
No one recognizes me here.
I move clandestinely. Free!
No one knows me here.

And then, at the end of the street,
a sharp right turn, second house,
third floor and two knocks.
No one knows me here. I am here.
Arrived. No one knows me here.

You wait, warm and strong. I enter
a tight space. For a brief moment.
Arrived! No one knows me here.

Your arms enclose me. I am here.
Arrived! No one, no one knows me
here. Only you and the sad smile
playing around your mouth
is loving. Is familiar.
I am here!

Confessions

I confess! I confess! I confess it all!
I loved. I lied. I LOVED!
It was not my fault! My heart is an
enemy of my head. I have tried
to synchronize my movements to lessons
taught a thousand times by faithful
and loyal servants of the past.

I confess! I did seek to deceive
those who knew better. I did
contrive to be alone. To sneak!
Yes! Sneak out. Sometimes I ran
out into the streets when all were
asleep. For shame. I confess.
I did crave the stolen moments
in a hidden place. But it was not
my fault.

Love is a body warm and loving. And
I did love warmly. I opened and I gave.
The private secrets of my body opened.
My heart is my enemy. In that room,
our self-imposed cell, we gave our
courage to each other. To bear those
moments of social deceit.

Yes, I am a traitor because I love without
reserve the body of my enemy. His arms
have held me. I have begged the kiss
of his lips that each time sank me deeper.
But, it was not my fault.

Chez toi

My doors have been shut so long
I am so acquainted with solitude.
Our understanding is such that
silence is all that is required.
We know tonight in *your* house
I will dine and dance alone.

It is by choice I tell you,
that my heart refuses to flutter.
My eyes blind to the sight of
invitations from others.
Your house is well cared for
and waiting in patience.

And I am sitting here
in my old rocking chair
knitting a new sweater
for you. Your pants are hung
and shirts are folded.
They wait and wait for you.

And when the barricades are torn
and water runs freely;
when teachers throw away
Misinformation—then
I shall pull back the
curtains of your kitchen.

And when freedom sounds loud
and guns are silent, my heart
shall open and your house
will be here . . . . waiting.
Waiting to receive you.

Alone

I shall miss your weight,
   your heavy hand holding me fast.
I shall miss your presence
    as I bathe, dress for bed
    in my bed encircling me.
I shall miss your kisses,
    your caresses, your voice
    in my ears.
I shall miss you when you go away.

When you go, my cup of coffee,
crumbs on my table cloth,
ring of wet from my sweat
drip glass, shall be consumed alone
without your comments on the news,
my schedule of postponed dates,
last minute entries or dinner time.

But I shall look inside my memories
and open a flood gate of times
when we were alone. Were together.

And I shall wait patiently for
the moment when you will fly out
of my heart. And I will remove
what I choose. Be content that
you were here with me.

António Jacinto (Angola)

Love Poem

> *También como la tierra*
> *yo pertenezco a todos.*
> *No hay una sola gota*
> *de odio em mi pecho. Abiertas*
> *van mis manos*
> *Esparciendo las uvas*
> *en el viento.*
>
> *(Like the earth, I belong to*
> *everyone. There is not a single*
> *drop of hatred in my breast.*
> *Open wide, my hands scatter grapes*
> *in the wind.)*
>
> —Pablo Neruda

When I return to see the sun's light they deny me
my love
we shall go dressed in peace
and wearing a smile of flowers and fruit
entwined
along roads—twisting snakes
among the coffee groves
climbing from the mountains to the stars
and to our shining dreams
we shall go
singing the songs that we know and do not know

When I return to see the sun's light they deny me
my love
we shall go
then go briefly to weep
on the countless graves of countless men
who have gone
without funeral or wake
without hope for the sun's light they deny us

We shall go, my love
and tell them
I have returned, we are returning
because we love each other
and we love
those countless graves of countless men.

When I return to see the sun's light they deny me
with standards raised
—freedom is a fruit of harvest—
we shall go
and gather corn cobs and colors
and offer flowers and resurrection to the dead
and to the living, the strength of our own lives
my love
we shall go
and draw a rainbow on the paper sky
for our son to play with:
    rain may come and rain may go
    if Our Lady wills it so
    rain for the father's farm will run
    and never, never send for the sun

We shall go, my love, we shall go
when I return
—the bars undone—
and embraced together we'll make
life, undeniable, continue
in the gentle gifts of harvest
in the chirping of startled birds
in the march of men returning
in the rains' hosannas on the reborn earth
in the confident steps of a people resolved
my love.

A fringe of new color will dress the earth
we shall make kisses and smiles the tissue of life
and between the endless cotton fields
and the dances of a joyful feast

we shall go
my love.

Translated from the Portuguese by Margaret Dickinson

Letter from a Contract Worker

I wanted to write you a letter
my love
a letter to tell
of this longing
to see you
and this fear
of losing you
of this thing which deeper than I want, I feel
a nameless pain which pursues me
a sorrow wrapped about my life.

I wanted to write you a letter
my love
a letter of intimate secrets
a letter of memories of you
of you
your lips as red as the *tacula* fruit
your hair black as the dark *diloa* fish
your eyes gentle as the *macongue*
your breasts hard as young *maboque* fruit
your light walk
your caresses
better than any that I find down here.

I wanted to write you a letter
my love
to bring back our days together in our secret haunts
nights lost in the long grass
to bring back the shadow of your legs
and the moonlight filtering through the endless
palms,
to bring back the madness of our passion
and the bitterness of separation.

I wanted to write you a letter
my love
which you could not read without crying
which you would hide from your father Bombo
and conceal from your mother Kieza
which you would read without the indifference
of forgetfulness,
a letter which would make any other
in all Kilombo worthless.

I wanted to write you a letter
my love
a letter which the passing wind would take
a letter which the cashew and the coffee trees,
the hyenas and the buffalo,
the caymans and the river fish
could hear
the plants and the animals
pitying our sharp sorrow
from song to song
lament to lament
breath to caught breath
would leave to you, pure and hot,
the burning
the sorrowful words of the letter
I wanted to write you.

I wanted to write you a letter
but, my love, I don't know why it is,
why, why, why it is, my love,
but you can't read
and I—oh, the hopelessness—I can't write.

Translated from the Portuguese by Margaret Dickinson

David Kerr (Malawi)

Elemental

The man above is supposed to rain
on the woman's cracked, hot earth.

But we have been so long tight-locked
drenching each other with love swirls,
we know neither plenty nor dearth,
up nor down, mortar/pestle, fool/
genius, hot/cold, pleasure/pain,
blue/brown, sun, cloud, hail or rock

but one fecund storm-pool
where all the elements whirl.

Swimming Pool Sacrament

My snorting serpent's
angle sees wind splash
the sky with spray plucked
away towards banana leaves'
ragged flutter, pulsing

like last night's wet-tight
grip of brown and white
limbs—snake-striped spasm—
plunged into crystal depths.

For this death, birth and fluid
life-growth by daytime
body turbine self unscrewing
is Extreme Unction, Baptism
and drum-slashed Passage Rite.

The Tattoo

You showed me the mark
(like equation signs)
inside your upper knees,
and told me the tattooist
warned it would make
besotted any man who
opened those thighs,
and you yelped in glee
at my mock-solemn sigh:
"It works!"

Wet and Dry

The deep pools of your river teem
with fish, water splashes plentifully
and rapids crash. My pitiful stream
clogged with "ifs" and "whens"
glugs into your mighty flow.

You blaze unconditionally, and cleanse
dusty rooms with your light; you refract
through wave-spray gratuitous rainbows,
while the shadows of my pale beams
creep from lunar crevices of the past.

My love is a desert flower, which fades
as stringy tendrils cling to cracked
rocks in search of lingering moisture,
yours is a vast Morula tree, generous
with sap and fruits, where my limbs
can stretch, grateful for the shade.

Go Crazy Over Me

Come here.
I want to pray for you.
Go crazy over me.

Don't act like you don't care.
Take off those clothes.
What do you have to lose?
I'm a free soul,
Never afraid to laugh.
Compassion lets me play
A slave or a king,
Happy to give away
All that's given to me.

What do you say?
Go crazy. It's ok.
Love is the only thing to do
And I know the way.

I don't want to complain
That water is too thin
And my shadow has run away,
Leaving me with lies,
Alone, bitter, vain
And going crazy too,
Since you're not crazy about me.

But don't worry.
My prayer is not really true.
If you really went crazy
I wouldn't know what to do.

Translated from Tigrinya by Charles Cantalupo and Ghirmai Negash

Daniel P. Kunene (South Africa)

Will You, My Dark-Brown Sister?

Dikerama: or, courting with "Grammars"
The following "grammars" are my recall, and poetic reformulation, of some of the colorful metaphors and images I remember being used by young men in courtship when I was a child. These young men, who had little or no schooling, had heard of something called "grammar," which was taught at school to reveal the richness of the language. Each created his own grammars. Often they bragged to each other about the number of grammars they knew, and a spontaneous competition might start to see who had the most grammars. Fresh ones might even be created on the spot.

I have decided to add a new (fictional) voice, that of the young woman who responds to the young man's pleas, something that would not happen in real life where she could only use body language.

I am a traveler
I am weary
I am hungry
Night has descended upon me
And I ask you, my sister, I say
Won't you open your door
And let me in?

> *You, a traveler who is weary*
> *who is hungry*
> *who is trapped in night's darkness*
>
> *I welcome you to rest under my roof*
> *to partake of meat and bread*
> *to come out of night's deep shadows*
> *and resume your journey in the morning.*

I would have passed your house, my sister,
On this long journey home
But I saw the storm clouds gathering
And I said to myself
"My sister lives here
My dark-brown sister

For whom, one day, the cattle in my father's kraal
Will bellow till the hills respond
She will take me in from the cold
And wrap a skin kaross around me."

I have come, my sister,
And am knocking on your door.

> *Yes, I saw the storm clouds gathering*
> *Flashes of lightning blinding my eyes*
> *I heard the thunder shaking the earth*
>
> *Come in, my dark-brown brother*
> *And rest a while*
> *Till the sky has spent its anger.*

I am like millet grains scattered on the ground
With no one to pick me up.
The birds are hovering over me
Ready to descend and gobble me up
With their beaks sharp as arrows.

Come, my sister,
Won't you gather me up and save me
From the anger of these hungry birds?

> *You shall not be food for the hungry hawks*
> *You who were destined to sink deep into the earth*
> *To make the earth pregnant with nourishment*
> *So life may return again and again*
> *And the circle not be broken*
> *Like the sun's rising and setting and rising and setting*
> *Darkness and light linking hands forever and ever*
>
> *I shall save you from the birds*
> *Place you in the granaries of time*
> *Till you can safely return to Mother Earth*
> *Where you belong*

I am the patient
You are the doctor

My heart is ill
My heart was wrenched from its place
And it went away like a cow to *mafisa*
When I saw you moving with the grace of a panther.

You, my sister, who induced my illness,
You have the healing herbs
To restore my heart to its place
For my heart slipped away
When I saw your brown body
Tall and straight like the stem of the *mohlwaare* tree
And I said to myself
The one who made my heart go away
Is the one who will restore it.

You are my *mmusapelo*, my dark-brown sister
You are my heart-restorer.

Come, coax my heart with love
And make it come back to its place.

> *Since I am the one who induced your illness*
> *Since I am the one who wrenched your heart from its place*
> *Since I am the one who made your heart to go to mafisa*
>
> *I shall, therefore, be your doctor*
> *I shall, therefore, be your heart-restorer*
> *And with healing herbs*
> *I shall coax your heart with love*
> *And make it come back to you*

Pick me up
Open your door and let me in
Wrap a skin kaross around me

Bring my heart back from *mafisa*,
And my father's cattle will bellow louder,
Point their horns towards your village,
And pierce the membrane of innocence
That separates you from me.

Music of the Violin

The gods favored me
In my moment of loneliness
Placed gently in my hands
A Stradivarius
Breathed into the Stradivarius and me
The knowledge to sing

I play first a pizzicato
With my nimble fingers
I pluck I pinch I twitch I tickle the strings
For naughty pleasures

Then up and down the scale
A gentle brush with the bow
And I tap and pat the sounding chamber

And, sensitive to a fault, the Stradivarius murmurs
Sweet strains like human voices falling from heaven
An anthem never before heard
Now the soothing strokes from my hands
Calm it to a gentle tempo

In the final strains,
The Stradivarius speaks to me
Entrances me with a diminished chord
That hovers tantalizingly over the precipice
Slides into a dominant chord
To deliver us into a tonic statement

And the music of the violin floats away
Floats away
Away. . . ..

To live forever
In the ensuing silence

It Is Not the Clouds

My Beloved
it is not the clouds
flitting across the moon
nor the few windowed lights
dotting the otherwise sleeping neighborhood

nor the floor beneath our feet
reminding us we're secure on this deck

it is not this cool air
first just a pleasant caress
then daring us with a few degrees of cold
till we said let's go inside

Nor is it the trees' soft love moans

or the stars hardly visible tonight

No, my Beloved
it is
neither the clouds
nor the moon
nor the nightly widowed lives
of sleeping neighbors
in their silhouetted houses
nor the breeze
nor the stars

But you
holding my hand
reflecting in your eyes
these interwoven meanings
that speak of love

Red

A little background to the poem below:
I find a mysterious red ladies' glove in my mailbox on campus. A note on the glove says "For Marcy" (note the spelling). Questions: Who? What? When? Why? race through my mind. A little bit of sleuthing determines that a male professor from the Slavic Department was the doer of the deed. Marci (not Marcy) had dropped it in his car when he drove her home. (His wife was present . . . I'm told!) A sort of midnight escape from the Prince's ball?

Red!
Stop!
Ask the question
that hangs in
the emptiness
of the red glove

Glove!
Red!
the emptiness
the question
"Oh glove where is thy hand?"

 "Did you, perhaps, slip off
in the midnight rush
when the princess and the charwoman
collided at the palace door?"

My mind is a landscape
of deserts and swamps and mountains
rivers and dense forests
which I traverse
mocked by ever-receding horizons
in search of the mysterious hand

No clues
red silence

and a name
on a slip
in an unknown hand

"Marcy!"

Liyongo Fumo (Kenya)

The Adventure in the Garden

In the name of God, I begin my story,
let me say what I want to say,
may I be led by my heart,
may the listeners be full of joy.

I was going out, going near a garden,
and I saw a tree, a young coconut palm,
and the guards who were guarding it,
were present, under a baobab tree.

I spoke to them: "You who are on guard,
give me one fruit of the tree."
They said: "Come up to our price!"
I said to them: "I will not give you what you ask."

One young boy appeared,
and climbed up to look for me,
for a reward, then he came back and told me,
"I have picked one fruit, the best one."

Why has this fruit not yet been eaten?
Like this one there are plenty in the bush;
And I pursued the snail's trail,
I felt neither worry nor sadness.

There the darkness began to spread,
and my heart told me: "Go on!"
I slid down from hill slopes and I climbed up,
and I arrived in my home.

Ode to Mwana Munga

Strike the buffalo horn
with the branch of berrywood or munga tree.

Blast the ivory horn
that resounds in the Sultan's palace,
let its echo reverberate
with the force of the elephant's voice.

Broadcast the echo,
let it rouse the sleeping families,
the women and the men,
let them hurry here in crowds.

Assemble the noble ladies, the dignified daughters,
and let them be seated here;
let us blend our verses
in praise of the Arabian lady.

Let us blend our verses,
and scan them carefully,
cast away the chaff
and retain the good ones.

Let us pause here,
arrange and refine our verses
till they are concise enough
to praise her delightful features.

My kinsmen, listen:
I shall start with her head,
her soft-silken hair
long-flowing and supple.

This noble woman's head
is as smooth as alabaster,

and well rounded
like a perfect circle.

Her ears
as she listens
curve out perfectly
like the blade of an anchor.

This lady's face, I swear,
I have yet to see its peer,
is beautifully molded
and blooms with its radiance.

Her matching eyebrows
are perfectly parallel
and neatly join at the root
as if they are knotted together.

Pitch-black,
darker even than ink,
they have joined hands
like arching acacia branches.

Whether she closes
or opens her eyes,
her countenance always fills
whoever is present with fear.

What a wonder her nose is;
its holes are visible
and number six
for he who counts them.

But do not be amazed,
if you look carefully,
twenty stars
are in her pupils.

Her cheeks,
fresh as coconut flesh
that yields squeezed oil,
surpass all others.

Her lips are thin
even when they are loosely closed;
whatever she utters
is lucid even to a simpleton.

Her teeth are lightning,
whiter than ivory
and as brilliant
as the Arabian lights.

Her tongue is as fiery
as the flame of a lantern;
it is especially radiant
whenever she recites the Koran.

Her mouth exudes
fragrant whiffs of the musk
of the civet perfume
from the wild or tame civet cat.

Her chin is rare, wonderful,
better than an almond,
more delicious than a cooked almond,
the Arabian Muscat nut.

Her neck is as long
as a noble bamboo
adorned with necklaces
neatly strung together.

Her shoulders are smooth;
they don't jut out

like glasses,
but they curve round.

Her armpits, my brothers,
where methinks a perfume tree grew,
will ravish a man
who sets his eyes on them.

The aroma that it exudes
is sweeter than jasmine
or the more fragrant
aloe oil.

Oh how I desire
her coral-colored nipples,
pink like the inner flesh
of the pomegranate.

I have neither witnessed
nor have I ever seen
such divine fruits
as those of the Arabian Lady.

Even inside the cloth
they already command respect,
and when they are bared,
a man's senses wander about.

Her belly is a cushion of flesh,
pleasant folds and secret nooks;
her navel is a gem that she can
retract and close like a cameo.

Her navel is the bowl of a water-pipe
crafted in Mecca;
anyone who inhales its perfume
will go dizzy with desire.

Heavy are her hips,
perfect for the game of finger
in the ring that has a gem
that clamps an inserted finger.

The sweetness of this clamp!
Captain, mind your compass needle!
Even without touching it,
it will begin to grip and squeeze.

Her little pool of fire,
when I saw it,
is neither long nor wide,
and it is full of juice.

It was cloudy and cool
with a soft pleasant breeze;
I carefully rigged up my dhow
and readied it for the voyage.

I unfurled the mainsail
made from ten mats
and very subtly
I pressed the bowsprit forward.

I turned the helm
and fitted the rudder;
I felt its strong pull in the water
as it glided towards Arabia.

So I entered the hold
to check for the bilge,
but after careful searching
I found no bilge water.

So I descended to the bottom
of the dhow, steered into the lagoon,

and when I reached the shore,
I blasted a cannon.

Its explosion blazed!
It reeked
a Meccan aroma
of the Arabian Lady.

When I inhaled her aroma,
I shuddered
as though from a cold
and went in search of healers.

The little dove's thighs
are like the butt of the royal clarion;
her girlfriends, eaten by envy,
curse her for it.

Her knees are special;
they are famous, celebrated
and well synchronized
as they turn around each other.

Her calves are moderate,
not too prominent,
but like a flute's mouthpiece
with a curved end.

The little rascal's foot soles
are covered by Indian slippers
of Arabian craftsmanship
ornamented with paintings.

Translated from the Swahili by Frank M. Chipasula

The Song of the Lotus Tree

To the Lady of the Lake I entrusted
My sapling of the lotus tree that I planted,
Shaded by the great iron mango tree,
In the fertile soil of her compound.

As my lotus sapling was sprouting straight up,
"Let us marry her off," they urged, ignoring me.
"Let us marry her off," they clamored without reason;
So I avoided her and I was depressed.

Without a suitor for her hand
Why would you give her away?
Together, you have excluded me;
Why, I ask, have you done so?

The lotus-tree is mine by birthright,
She is mine by divine inheritance,
A legacy from my guardian,
from the God of all Creation.

Listen all as I shower praises upon this tree
whose seed comes from Arabia;
God's providence granted me this seed
That descended from Yemen.

Let me praise before you, my kinsmen,
This lady superior in grandeur and glory
whose pedigree mocks any heavenly light
like the moon shining in the sky.

She will be a pleasure to her husband
whom she will fill with great joy;
and he will return here laughing,
praising God the Beneficent.

He will praise the Lord joyously;
they will share pleasant laughter,
while smiles grace their lips
and joy gladdens their hearts.

He will pray to God for increase
that He may populate the tree of paradise
whose fruits resemble the apricot,
the wild or Mediterranean pomegranate.

When the damp cool wind murmurs,
she will sway like a youthful bamboo,
and her leaves will resemble emerald,
an incomparable green color.

When its flower begins to bloom,
even a jewel will be as worthless
as Venus, dawn's constant star,
when day is about to dawn.

And when its fruit swells with ripeness,
Its perfume is pleasant and aromatic;
It appears neither too big nor too small,
its surface harmonious and smooth.

Its peel is as soft as doe's pelt,
Its leaves fluffy as birds' feathers;
the fruit and the flower's fragrance
is better than musk and saffron.

When a man picks and kisses her,
She will withdraw timidly into herself;
And when he harvests and eats her,
she will ease his burning desire and distress.

Though the man who picks it may be sane,
its sweetness, which surpasses Turkish delight,

will drive him completely crazy.
Rejoice then in this gift from God the Giver.

Sugarcane is the grass of choice;
it transports a man into rare delights.
Here I end praising the sapling
Of the tree from paradise,
That has no peer upon this earth.

Translated from the Swahili by Frank M. Chipasula

Lindiwe Mabuza (South Africa)

A Love Song

It was good
The orchestral dance
Of our voices sipping dew
In the soft morning-rise
Of Africa south.
That was good.
We welcomed with a squeeze
The hand of desire as it dabbled and dappled
A summer mosaic
Across the canvas of thighs
Which swallowed the embrace
Of live dreams
It was good.

Now we swim in warm-baths
Of our nakedness,
Touching with our skin
The subterranean regions
Of our blood.
We move with the heave of time
Whose mouth is a fenceless water-fall
Stretching,
Turning some,
Now mellowing in one, with one.

It was good,
When tears watered the corpses
From the storage of past tales,
And tears circled their death
Above the face
Of the come of love
That was good.

Then we sponged
The ache of each beat
With the blend of hope
In sunbeam eyes
As I saw mine mirrored in yours.

Another Song of Love

In your loneliness
your hurt eyes warmed to my love.
In your glum
you said I was a sunbeam.
we hopped in and out
of each other's heart and mind
to nurse and nurture our young plant.

Then came days of revelry.
Your time was full, too full
sometimes I thought
except for a civil gesture waved at me
from time to time.
I genuflected at the altar
of your heart,
with gifts of me;

You backed away because you had not
counted
on my tenacious love grips.
With the spirits of our beginnings
Inebriated by other spirits
you prefixed frowning titles
to my name.

In my loneliness
I could not reach you.
In my love
you saw your smothering mother.
But because I was not,
your shadow grew more distant
with the setting sun.

Now your burnt ashes float
to mingle with others.
And as I wait for another day
I keep singing another song
How did I go astray!

Shanghai Suite

(Our one heart)

If I should completely
Cease to breathe
Right now
Especially
After last night's tenderness
Please bury my heart
Where neither wind
Sun
Rain
Nor maggot
Can dare to feed
On all such treasure kists

Because wherever I venture
In this tropical haven
Your presence turns
Each breadth of mind
Each breath
Into chimes that
Encircle our entire being
With irresistible
Currents
Our charged bodies receive
As they venture to give
Sighs that write
Countless
Warm thoughts

So that
Beloved
Even in this separation
I am drawn
So close to your baton

That the tempo
In the pulse
Beats closer
Then pulls
Drawing
To such pure pitch
This timbre
That defies
Any intrusion
Or curious stares
Whenever we allow ourselves
To be spirited
Into a realm
Made
Just for us

Thus
Now
I plead after delicious death
That we rest our
New heart
In the labyrinth
Of some high mountain shade
Where it must
Triumph over centuries
Whose star-crossed lovers
Will come to
Measure how
Each weight
Each gram
Grain or atom
In our preserved mummy
So totally mixed
Bonding us into
Soul-blooded mates in this
Our one heart

Jacarandas for Love

How could I not think of you
Wherever you might be right now
Today
This day that perfectly mixed
Sun wind and vast blue
With Jacarandas cast
In fullest bloom
Their most delicate short spell
Stretched in arched canopy of sweet lavender
In matrimonial splendor
Along lavish Harare lanes
Where purest fragrance baits and bathes senses
In profuse delight

It is especially in this solo soul's paradise
I wish you here
Where the mad stampede of time
Unearths roots that so deeply long
To abandon forever the ember of single flights
When even canaries flood above the head
And such vivid gentle splashes
Force the heart to pulse and swell
With yet another warm hunger
To lay itself bare
Along the spring of your mellow blood
And nurse that vacant season
Vagrant for fulfillment wrapped in embrasures
In the soft tremble of your soothing tears
And the laughter of moans and groans dancing
Whispered in enchantment of mating nights
Where Jacarandas await to bless
With soft petals
Unloved lovely loveables alike
Alive.

Long-Distance Love

If we had our country
To mold in our hands
So that this soft clay could shape the face
And heart of freedom
Each toll on love
Each tick of distance
Could be some blessing
For I would have
The rare fortunes of a bird
After every mission abroad
All encounters with foreigners
Would reinforce the reason
Turning the strange into loveliness
The urgent to certainty
Of reunion more desirable
For like the birds
Nightfall would kindly lead
To favored nests
To recount encounters
Hatch new flights
Till together we can soar
To heights where such long-distance throbs
Which may pulse pain
Are ever foreign
Being alone will be forever alien.

Kristina Masuwa-Morgan (Zimbabwe)

This Morning

This morning I visited the place where we
lay like animals
O pride be forgotten
And how the moon bathed our savage nudity in purity
And your hands touched mine in silken caresses
And our beings were cleansed as tho by wine.
    Then you stroked my breast
And thro' love I shed the tears of my womb
O sweet fluid spilled in the name of love
O love
O sweet of mine existence
Your sigh of content as your lips touched my soul
O joy shared by the wilderness
O gentle breeze
O fireflies that hovered over our nest in protective
    harmony
How I yearn
I feel you here again with me.
See how the flowers, the grass, even the little shrubs have
    bloomed
Even as I bloomed under the warmth of your breath
And now they look at me; unashamed
For they have been washed and watered by the love
    of your loins.

I stretch and sigh in warm contemplation
For tonight I shall again possess you
In me, I shall be content of all you render
On account of love
Under the stars I shall drink the whisperings of your body
Speak again to the depths of my sensibility
Tree of my life

Peaceful meadows
Cow dares not moo here
Ruler of the night
Lord dynamo
Let me not disturb your peace
But let me lie with you again
Be silent O silence
Love has found its awakening

Farewell Love

All I have to give is this loving thought
A love that gold nor diamonds can buy
Held out by a hand of love; no gloves
Pure in its composition;
That no dictionary of phraseology can bespoil
Wrapped up with love
With naught asked in return
No acclamations nor favors
But to understand
This love I have always felt, will always know.
We left many questions unasked
Many kind words unsaid
And harmony failed us
But my part was always love
And thro' that love I shall remember only the times we
    loved
And hope to you
That when times start getting rough
You shall think only of the times we called each other friend
And hope shall bring us one day together again
There will again be
The fights,
Reproach after reproach
Inferiority and guilt shall again be inflicted
And experiments on feelings of neglect
And harmony shall again fail us
Yet forever love
A love that was born in a mother's womb we shared
To friendship and sistership
Adios!

Timeless Love

Never again will this moment be ours
My mind be filled with such certainty
And fires burn my being with love
Impeccable genie of love
Bottled at the core of mine existence
For cloud hanging over tree
—Green tree
Soft, kind and patient cloud
White, pure and understanding . . .
Cloud hanging over the silent afternoon
Cloud stilled by Godly sanctity
Watchful over the fire within me
Sunlight, starlight, candlelight and heat
Painless rocks and warm breeze . . .
Yet pain and misery unavoidable
For just like that cloud
You shall at the end of this day depart
And this moment of peace will be but a memory.

We Part . . .

the lorry driver's stressful glare
arms still jolt akimbo,
next to him his iron monster
—Munya lies still
a smile lingers on His face hardly formed
i remember how his lips once whispered to mine
when we languished in love's esteem

i still love you Munyaradzi
though Your arm is crushed and gone
Your sides like the breasts of age unbodiced
the crowds steam in, hardly summoned,
greasy heads peer through masses of humanity
You despised them so
stares grip Your heaped past
yet You lie undisturbed
beneath the tatters of Your clothes
which this morning You so earnestly pressed
i visualize Your caring face glowering
So much life You were owed
such promise
Your face still shines
You lie there unhearing
proud like an everlasting pedagogue
eyes open, watching, seeing naught
at last You sleep.
go home
i've taken You this far
You leave me
An infant crying for its mother
Your memory will always remain
a cancer swelling within me,
go home Munyaradzi
the children call,

go home
the coach waits
they think they cover shame
go home
i follow close behind.

Makhokolotso K. A. Mokhomo (Lesotho)

When He Spoke to Me of Love

The day he first spoke to me of love
The day he taught me in those words,
The marvel in my breast, and dreams,
I dreamed even in the middle of the day.
My voice was burnt away, a fire
In my throat licked at my words—
In my pride I stood there quite dumb,
All my face wet with happy tears.
Fear struck fast and heavy at my side
That he might change, and barking dogs
Drive off the bridal cattle brought for me.
I came trembling to him on my knees
As if stooped down in a prayer of love.
My beloved, his voice more sweet,
His young mouth poured a stream of gold.
My great one, he looked long into my face
And my tongue, unstrung, confessed to him.

I Want to Be All Things to You

I want to be with you
Like a grafted branch;
I want to be your dark rind
Close to the bark.
When the whirlwind locks you in
I want to be your taproot so you are not restless.
I want to be your sunshine
Your fountain in the drought
Your lute I will be
To voice your deepest thought.
I want to be all things to you
And you to be my wife,
But, go ahead, spit in my face!
One day you will be mine.

Maria's Photograph

The beauty of my love is the rainbow colors
Of sun's rays in dewdrops (only more radiant)
Eliciting echoes from the stars.
Her eyes sparkle like diamond's sparkles
Her neck is balanced like a giraffe's,
Her poise is majestic like a palm tree unswaying.
Yet stars are endurable
Like the firmaments they are
While my love's beauty is brittle like glass
That at a snap shatters into a thousand bits;

Mr. Photographer, take a picture of Maria,
Frame the image for me to keep
That captures those features I admire:
The glitter in her eyes, the crystal in her teeth,
The twinkling smiles that reach to the moon,
Brown earth her skin, soignée black her hair
Glistening as she tills the rain-washed garden . . .
Please, take a picture of Maria
And frame it for me to keep;

But a photograph fades with time
Edges chip, frame wastes,
Sheen rubs off with constant hands,
And the texture of Maria I admire
Will relapse into the brown-grey of age.
I would rather weave Maria into song
Hummed whenever this page is sung,
I would sing her features for ever.

Search for a Bride

Lubani lavender will give her away,
Or else her melodious voice.
I will move in ivory light at dawn,
Comb ridge after ridge of the green landscape,
For I am the shell-necklace lover of the hills,
Intent on finding Tasiyana for a bride.
Only the speckled pigeon's cooing
Can explain to me now, note by note,
Why I should stop the search for my bride.
I will know her, I am certain,
By the mark of her bracelet,
The sunspots on her freckled face
And the sheen of her shell necklace.
I will woo her with the nimble feet of an *ingoma* dancer,
I will unlace her sunbrown mountain sandals, and
Untie her loin cloth of black, red and green,
Bright like flames on the lake,
And I will engulf her with the fire of my loins.
But should any mortal come between her and me,
I will turn to the sun and blind her with my blood.

The Feet of a Dancer

for Natasha, watching her play the viola

Some healer, perhaps, in the magic of her past,
taught her to sing in unison with the seasons.
Neck outstretched, preening as a locking wagtail,
unfettered, hands flicking, she plays the harp and sings.

Then she starts dancing. I say
it is her soul, those feet, as nimble in grace
as a gazelle's in the Savannah. Her gait glazed in the dim light,
her feet rapping, she rises, widely framed beauty.

My eyes flutter and I fly back many years to Thoza:
the green brooks where I grew up, where
neighbors and game share the same spaces,
in a flash I fly twenty-some years and recall

Another dancer: glazed in the wind, turning to her *vimbuza* dance,
she raps into ankle-bells, pausing,
waiting for the call of my drum, poised,
walking rows of gleaming initiates—what can I do
but let linger my gaze on the luminous flush of her nipples.

I say: I have heard your voice in the fields at home,
and I call it the scented sun flowers of the veld,
the creek orchids in bloom
before they extinguish their thunder-red life.

I say: I have seen your feet cut up the plateaux,
and I call them rivulets and groves of the veld,
water that colors and livens the land, flowing
from thunder, which is the sound your dance makes.

Waiting for You

The orange light of dawn
Reflected morning dew
Doused our faces blank,
Stripped all colors from ochre-painted walls
Jutting into space like crops of rock.

We watched sunbirds break the quiet of morning,
And against the same fire-red backdrop of dawn
I wanted to feel the long curves of your body,
Your hands wrapped around mine,

Your sweet whispers soothing the rough edges
Of my mind, erasing all doubts of your love.
And here, if I thought it would make you smile,
I would point out our shadow against the wall,

Point out that fullest side of the moon
That changes the tide, our dark companion
That'll never walk away from us. Yearning for you,
I intend to live fully by it.

Muyaka bin Haji (Kenya)

A Poem to His First Wife

I would rather have the small boat,
my first little vessel,
although it was unsteady and shaky,
the waves never rose above her head;
but she drowned near Ngozoa
on a dark night.
That is what I am thinking about today,
it makes me feel confused and numb.

My little boat, my seaworthy boat,
when I first made it float on the water,
it was full of playfulness,
and I was pleased and charmed by it;
I crossed over on it to the other shore,
and the waves did not rise above it.
That is why today I am thinking about her,
it makes me feel confused and numb.

Male lions and elegant ladies,
listen, I have something to say:
I spurned the villages
and the voyages in a small craft;
today I remember the beautiful boat
on which I could hoist and lower the sails.
Oh, the gift and the receiver,
When it will meet him.

Oh, the receiver and the gift,
the gain that gives a man his growth!
Although she was a small child
of timid character, yet she inspired respect;

there was great benefit in her,
she longed for austerity.
Oh, illness and recovery,
when the latter meets the former.

Oh, health and sickness,
the one who has the latter becomes ugly,
he goes a long, long way,
in order to find good health;
when he finds that it is over for him,
he wants to go and show himself happily.
Oh, the soul and life
when they meet.

Oh, life and the soul,
when life is finished for a mortal,
he praises the Lord,
that is a good thing, it adorns him;
on the Last Day, before God,
may the path to Paradise not throw him off.
Oh, paradise and the mortal soul,
when they meet.

Oh, the mortal soul and paradise,
when he first settles down in it,
he will ask for favors
of the Prophet who forgives;
what he likes he will see
with all that he desires.
Oh, joy and the heart,
when they at last will meet!

When We Shall Meet, You and I!

If my messenger arrives,
my representative from Mombasa,
he will come with a letter,
a very good one, and bring it to you;
or in case he should deliver it orally,
he would speak the words to you.
But there is no way
of seeing you personally.

But there is no way
of seeing the bright light of your face,
so I am postponing
coming to you for a visit.
No penetrable place to penetrate
can I see with my eyes,
so I am undetermined,
and unable to meet you.

So I am undetermined what to do;
otherwise I should already have appeared,
without feeling dissatisfied with myself,
I cleared my conscience, I would go;
but I fear the guards
who are on duty all the time.
So I checked myself
and did not go to see you.

So I checked myself,
although my heart could not bear it;
I tried to persuade my heart away from love,
after that I even tried to make it forget.
I am not afraid to put pressure on it,
so as to reduce its longing for you,
its longing that results from missing the light
of seeing you.

Because of missing the light,
that brightness that continues shining,
I see a great darkness all the time,
wherever I turn my gaze.
Do not think that it pleases me to stay away,
it was not for that reason that I refused to come!
I am in love, I cannot forget
the hope of seeing you again.

I am in love, I have not forgotten
my beloved friend.
You accepted me out of kindness,
with compassion and grace.
How could I wish to stay away from you
today, these days or any other time?
How can I refuse
to see you?

How could I refuse
to come to you, my little turtle-dove?
You are the crown-pearl in the necklace
which it would be a joy to string!
It dispels sadness
at the moment I put it on.
Deserting you would be folly;
not to see you would be impossible for me.

To let you go would be impossible,
foolishness forever;
but you must watch your honor,
it is not a negligible thing.
And to go as far as to spoil that
is a thing I refuse to do.
But do not think I had an aversion
to seeing you again.

Do not think I had an aversion,
you graceful beauty,
child of pure superior stock,
without stain or blemish!
I did no evil things,
otherwise you would have been dishonored.
I will love your appearance
when you and I meet!

The Shawl

You, my letter on Syrian paper,
go about it in a white man's way;
go to that good Muslim woman,
that woman who does good works for God!
When you have greeted her,
speak to her with humility,
take me and my friends,
"Give me my shawl!"

My shawl that makes such a rich rustling noise,
which I gave you as a present;
I was surprised to learn that you were wearing it,
while you were going round in search of men.

I did not know, when I first met you,
that things would be like this;
now take off that shawl at once,
and give it back to me.

That place where you go every night, my girl,
when the sun has set,
you do not hear the call to prayer,
because you are carried away by love.
Tell your friend to go to the market,
he will buy one just like this;
don't stop taking it off,
and give me my shawl.

Even if I borrowed money for it,
I shall pay its price eventually.
The custom with a debt is that one pays;
even you know these things.
Greedy female,
gradually your body will become ugly.

You and me, no remedy will cure our relationship,
I want my shawl.

Give it to me personally, at once,
before disgrace descends on your head.
I, Muyaka, will not be deceived,
Don't you try and cheat me.
When we first met, I had no suspicions,
and I expected that we would stay together,
but now, at least, you have been useful to me,
let me have my shawl.

If you say I have no use for it,
I will send it to my mother;
this is just the thing she loves,
she will go and wrap herself in it.
As for you, I am afraid of you,
I cannot let you have it.
I will not let you have a cubit,
give me my shawl.

In the Village

for Nosipho

Daughter of our unforgotten ancestral chain
When you hear a bird singing in the tree
It is singing our traditional love song
About the good rains we had through the years
About our good harvest we longingly remember

Daughter of our unforgotten ancestral chain
My love feelings for you flew out of my hut today
Destined for your father's far-away homestead
Bringing good news about our destined togetherness
That will make every villager happy to have a feast

Daughter of our unforgotten ancestral chain
We shall bring you bracelets made from copper
Designed by the master blacksmith of the village
For your majestic beautifully created arms
Plus of course our joint creative designs.

Desert Sandwich

The gods must have created my land with a purpose
To give the colonial conquerors a fatal dose
If along the Skeleton Coast they dared to pose
For a portrait or grow a multi-colored rose
Here they died of thirst or bled through the nose
Thus, just make an attempt and we'll ceaselessly oppose.

The gods must have created my land with a purpose
To leave me with my less-demanding spouse
Her vase empty without a yellow or red rose
Yet when the rains come our soil gets a dose
From Mother Nature that's more than a rose
For she'll abundantly expose.

The gods must have created my land with a purpose
When hunting I always carefully chose
My arrow smeared with a deadly dose
To kill a selected animal, never to arouse
Suspicion amongst those as elders pose
Protectingly what the gods created with a purpose.

António Agostinho Neto (Angola)

A Bouquet of Roses for You

(On Maria Eugénia's birthday)

A bouquet of roses for you
—roses red white
yellow blue—
roses for your day

Softness and freshness
in the anxious curves of the earth
and the poetic exaltation of life
—softness and freshness for your day

The joy of friendship
in the cheerless grimace of death
and on the catalyzing sap of affection
joy and friendship for your day

And on your day
in me too a melting
of anxieties and emotions
of sadness and anger
of certainty and faith
and all the tiny shades of varied life
mingled in the kaleidoscopes of the horizon
and all hopes

A bouquet of roses for your day

The fraternal embrace of the setting sun
and of the nascent moon
the urgent defeat of the old
and the growth of the new
in each step of the days
in each hour of the days

in each of your smiles;
all shades of matter
aridity of deserts
and fecundity of founts
grace of tigers
and docility of doves
fury of rivers
wrath of winds
and disconcerting human variation
hatred and love
yellow smiles in the hypocrisy of souls
cries moans abundance and misery
all gathered
in the bouquet of roses
for your day

The bitter taste of imminent spring
comes pregnant with force
comes full of despair
and frustration
and no possible defeat
can dethrone the force conveyed
in the bitter taste of imminent spring
and in each one of your days

Force and certainty
in the bouquet of roses
for your day

And the place conquered on earth
by the men of machines
and super-sound
through fraternity
and through friendship
shall always be theirs
and also yours and ours

even if waters leap from their beds
and eroded mountains
release the winds

A place conquered
in the bouquet of roses
for your day

A bouquet of roses for you
—roses red white
yellow blue—
roses for your day
and Life!—for your day

Tenderly I wrap them
in the fleeting yearning
of a brief winter.

Translated from the Portuguese by Marga Holness

Two Years Away

Greetings—you say in yesterday's letter
when shall we see each other
soon or later
tell me love?

In the silence
are the talks we did not have
the kisses not exchanged
and the words we do not say
in censored letters

Against the dilemma of today
of being submissive or persecuted
are our days of sacrifice
and audacity
for the right
to live thinking to live acting
freely humanly

Between dreams and desire
    when shall we see each other
    late or early
    tell me love!
more justly even grows
the longing to be
with our peoples
today always and ever more
free free free

Translated from the Portuguese by Marga Holness

Gabriel Okara (Nigeria)

Silent Girl

Sweet silent girl
what makes you speak not
what makes you speak not
of our days, and the days before?
what makes you speak not but only in silence
with your lips tight and tongue pressed against
your teeth by your pressing thoughts?
Is it because of the sneering, nagging present?
the present that has scorched yams, corn and minds,
the present that has turned babies into adults
and adults to babies, babbling babies
learning how to crawl and walk—
the present that has turned night sounds
of rural peace to sounds of exploding shells
and rattling guns and raucous laughter of death
and days of promise to heavy heart crushing days;
The present that has dried us all of emotion
and the youth of youth like harmattan the trees of living sap.
Let's break with the past that bred the present
and let today be reminder of tomorrow
though tomorrow may only be a dream
as dream may vanish in our waking
or may survive—you, the silent one or me who sings.
So be silent sweet girl
I'll be silent, speak in silence,
and let's recline on tomorrow of our dream
in the shadows of our silent thoughts
away from the hot sneering days.

To Paveba

When young fingers stir
the fire smoldering in my inside
the dead weight of dead years rolls
crashing to the ground
and the fire begins to flame anew,

The fire begins to flame anew
devouring the debris of years—
the dry harmattan-sucked trees,
the dry tearless faces
smiling weightless smiles like breath
that do not touch the ground.

The fire begins to flame anew
and I laugh and shout to the eye
of the sky on the back of a fish
and I stand on the wayside
smiling the smile of budding trees
at men and women whose insides
are filled with ashes, who
tell me, "We once had our flaming fire."

Then I remember my vow.
I remember my vow not to let
my fire flame any more. And the dead
years rise creaking from the ground
and file slowly into my inside
and shyly push aside the young fingers
and smother the devouring flame.

And as before the fire smolders in water,
continually smoldering beneath
the ashes with things I dare not tell

erupting from the hackneyed lore
of the beginning. For they die in the telling.
So let them be. Let them smolder.
Let them smolder in the living fire beneath the ashes.

To a Star

1

I strain my tired voice in song
to reach up to the star by the moon
a song I vowed never more to sing;
But from sundown to sunrise
I seek a union continually
which breaks my vow and I sing
a silent song to the rhythm of ageing drums
drums not heeding constraints of fear
Bear the song tenderly toward the ear

But enfeebled by layers of falling years
the muted song reaches not the star

Still with a beggar's persistence I sing
vainly seeking harmony with song and drum
drum waxing louder, fed by each passing day
But it echoes only in the hills of dead years
and reaches not the STAR by the moon

Yet I dare to hope for a confluence of songs
    Mine enfeebled, sluggish
    The STAR's bright, engulfing
This song of creation in my head revolving

2

Who can stop this sacred song
that chains heart to heart?
this song that defies the seer
    hard to hear?
This song that forbids discord
but thrives in lasting accord?

O let not this be as those
which lie scotched like rose
trampled by passing years
Before it reaches the STAR

3

I am tired, tired!
my trembly feet drag.
Those in blood-bond
pass me by in their dream
And I, chastened by their passing
Drag my tired feet along
in pursuit of my own dream.

Celestial Song

1

Your song is celestial song
and so in "different plane"
mine is terrestrial song
and so is vain
vain, but it seeks ceaselessly
like rushing water the sea.
Let yours come down in drips
in crystal drips of starry light
to illumine the approaching night.

2

My song vainly climbs
like smoke from humble hearths.
It rises from lowly depths
to reach up to your song
but it is muffled by racing clouds.
So let yours come down in drips
just in drips, drips of starry song
To strengthen my trembly feet.

Mohammed Said Osman (Eritrea)

Juket

Juket broke up with me and left.
I don't know why.
Not enough love? Another guy?
What can I do?

Curse God and die?
I can't get her out of my head.
I feel beat up.
Happiness is being dead

And not in love.
Will she ever want me again?
Maybe one of my poems would make
Juket listen?

> *Juket, I'm your faithful dog,*
> *On guard and coming when you say.*
> *Tell me to follow and I will*
> *Only seeing your body sway,*
> *Not caring if my legs fall off.*
> *I'll hold on by your eyelashes*
> *And eyes as sharp as the gazelle's.*
> *Your teeth and smile will bathe my soul*
> *Like milk and keep me out of hell.*
> *Letting your long hair tumble down*
> *Your round breasts to your narrow waist,*
> *You know I'm starving for a taste.*
> *Wine beads the bottle of your neck.*
> *It's like a spring I want to drink.*
> *I'm like a wasp, but you're the sting*
> *All the way down, pointing your legs*
> *And up to the chocolate cake*
> *Of your cheeks, where I breathe new life.*

Maybe something like this will bring
My Juket back
And she will sing
I see you suffering. Enough.

If not, I'm stuck
Out in the cold
With no one and nothing to make
Life worth living.

Translated from Tigre by Charles Cantalupo and Ghirmai Negash

Words Catch Fire

Words catch fire
On the bliss of the moment
As I stalk my way through
The forbidden territory between your legs
The beckoning petals of your eyes
The succulent eternity of your warm, obliging lips . . .
Touching legs, tangled tales
Delicious softnesses, desires so divine!

My will is a whisper, your moan a method
I, your sin,
Committed between two holy mountains
And a valley of carnal angels

Puzzle

What should I do to gain your nod

Should I lie like a politician
        swagger like a soldier
        prattle like a poetaster

Should I lay absent fortunes at your door
        rob a bank
        poach forget-me-nots from an enemy's garden

Should I stand on my head
        sleep with eyes open
        pen your praise in blood

Should I send the wind to your roof
        lace your leisure with imps
        ask *sigidi** to dance for you

Should I become your slave
        run your every errand
        your chain golden iron around my neck

           Or

Should I charm you with my songs
        lead you by the quiet waters
        get your dream to yes my plea?

              * Yoruba effigy feared for its mischief.

Divine Command

"What must I do?" I ask,
"before I throw my hands around your waist?
What must I do
before I inherit the queendom of your softness?"

"Raise your hand," you say,
"and pluck me the moon;
go down to the sea
and bring my buried jewel

Cook my yam
with the fire of a cockscomb;
set me a-sail
on the spittle of an ant

Make my drum
with the prepuce of a prince;
sing me a song
from the fair of fairies."

You Are

You are my Earth
    my root, my roost

The roof above my dreams
    fireplace for my frozen feelings

You are the Temple of my Desire
    with a thousand inner rooms and a thousand echoes

You are the race
    which lends a name to my legs

The infinite destination
    shepherdess of my nomadic fancies

You are the Rain
    which fell before the sky

My flood, brown every moon
    with pagan promise

You are the river rippling coastwards
    with tales of upland regions

My sea of blue songs
    capering clams and dancing minnows

You are the smoke
    which blends with my evening sky

My horizon of infinite past
    and liquid futures

You are a song so sweet in its tempting distance
    my ears yearn for the magic of your softness

Love in a Season of Terror

I wanted so much to come
but there were corpses across the path

The Generals, drunk on beer and blood,
emptied mortar shells into surging crowds,
in desperate awe of a foe called Democracy.

Loud was the chaos which became our noon;
the sun took cover behind a phalanx of clouds
the great *odan* tree was a fog of scream and smoke

Oh how gravely your absence unclothed my heart!

These, precious one, are seasons of terror.
Criminals in khaki have seized the streets
weighted down by a mess of medals

Their muftied cronies, robes flowing,
parade tongues filed into fangs
by venal licking of boots . . .

How does one love in times like these, Beloved:
with bazookas coming between our lips,
the General threatening us with the bayonet

Between
his
legs?

Tender Moment

And you smile your big-cheeked smile,
Your eyes breaking out of your face
Like the sun through the mist
Of a young and ancient dawn;

Your lips play around the base
Of your teeth,
A laughter erupts, fresh
As the frothy song of a mountain stream

Finding rippling echoes
In the hard-soft depth of unseen things
And the fable of inchoate showers
Which tease the thighs of sprawling fancies

Your eyes memorize the hours,
Stretch dry moments into succulent eternities
Then run them d-e-e-p
Like the Zambezi of our rooted longings

You are the fragrance
Which lends a name to varnished gardens,
The door to which hums the chronicle
Of the house . . .

And so you said:
  "Let us go behind the walls
    And I will show you
      The birthmark below my navel"

Jean-Joseph Rabéarivelo (Madagascar)

There You Are

(from *Translations from the Night*)

There you are
standing straight and bare!
You are mud and you remember it;
but truly you were born of the parturient darkness
that feasts on lunar lactogen;
slowly then the trunk in you took shape
above this little wall that dreams of flowers clear
and the scent of waning summer.

To feel, to think that roots sprout from your feet
and run and twist like thirsty serpents
toward some subterranean stream,
or fix themselves in sand
and bind you to it even now,
you, O living,
unknown, unassimilated tree,
who swell with fruits that you yourself will gather.

Your summit
of hair tousled by the wind
conceals a nest of insubstantial birds
and when you come to share my bed
and I recognize you, O my errant brother,
your touch, your breathing, and the odor of your skin
will rouse the sound of mystic wings
until we cross the border into sleep.

Translated from the French by Ellen Conroy Kennedy

from Old Songs of Imerina Land

Imaginary tremolo.
The daughter had come to meet me
When her parents took the notion to prevent it.
I spoke soft words to her.
She did not answer.
You will grow old there, you and remorse:
We and love
Shall go home to our house.

Thursdays for he-who-has-good-fortune,
Fridays for he-who-has-a-sweetheart.
Bring me strong tobacco
To chew as a digestive;
Bring me gentle sayings
That I may root my life in them.
Let come what may.
If my father and mother must die
I must find an amulet to bring back life;
If my love and I must part
May the earth and sky be joined.

The wife of another, O my elder brother,
Is like a tree that grows by a ravine,
The more one shakes it, the more it takes root,
Take her at night, take her in the evening,
Only he who takes her
May have her altogether.

Poor blue water lilies:
All year long up to their neck in tears,
Blades of water grass,
Reeds, rushes, ponds dragged by canoes,
Give me sanctuary, I am so unfortunate!
Steal a bit of love for me: I am another's.

Delight in your wife.
He who has no pepper
Takes no delight in eating.
He who loses his fishing net
Will have nothing to fry.
And I, if I lose you,
Will lose my nearest kinsman.

XVIII

Close by, to the north, there were two oranges: one was ripe, the other
so beautiful it made one happy. I gave the ripe fruit to the Cherished
One and the one-so-beautiful-as-to-bring-happiness to the Beloved.
But I cherish the one and truly love the other in vain. If either had a
passion to subdue me, I would not know what to do.

XLVII

—May I come in? May I come in?
—Who is there? Who is it?
—It is I, the first born of my mother and my father.
—The first born of his mother and his father. The one who wears
brightly colored clothes and carries high his head? The one who hops
into his shoes and goes to lie inside his litter? In that case, come in,
young man: the calf is neatly tied, and my father and my mother are
away. But if you're seeking robes as fine as wings of dragonfly or locust,
look elsewhere. And if you come for short-lived love, I'd rather give you
up before than after.

LVII

A wife is like a blade of grass: she stands upon her feet but is easily
withered. A husband is like a clump of seaweed: he flourishes in water
but is easily shredded.
—Young man, how many loves have you?
—I have hardly any, cousin, for they are only seven: the first, who cuts
my fingernails; the second, who takes over for the one who stays at home
when we go out; the third, who replaces the second in emergencies;
   the fourth, who follows me with longing eyes when I depart; the

fifth, who comes to meet me when I return; the sixth, who nourishes my life as much as rice; the seventh, who doesn't mix with the crowd, and even if she does, always manages to make herself distinguished.

Translated from the French by Ellen Conroy Kennedy

Jacques Rabémananjara (Madagascar)

The Lyre with Seven Strings

You will follow me, pale Sister,
Chosen before the dawn of the world!
Bride when the earth was still without form and void
Sole reason of the Creation! Power of my destiny!

You will come.
Vain
Will be the cries of your blood, the grumbling pride of your race.

You will follow me.
March of love! Flight of the dove!
O Freshness of the first morning!

Your brothers
Have grown deaf,
insensible even to the smell of powder, to the fury of the thunder.

Harder
than granite their hearts drunk with carnage and death.

The sweetness of your message, my sister,
has only moved the myriad ranks
of the stars,
only moved my primitive soul,
mirror and sole reflection of your lot.

They have understood nothing
in the tumult of the massacre, in the glowing of the fires.
Folly
has galloped
whinneying
from the entrails of the abyss to the rent summit of space and sky.

Yet from the four points of the horizon
arise
the sounds of a trumpet and curves of your high
melodies,
O Peace!
Daughter of the dolorous Earth!
Image of the Loved-one, honey of spring on the blue
    banks of Assoussiel.

You will come, pale Sister, to the country of dreams, to the banks
    of royal springs.
White, white the orchid at the peak of the Hill of Alassour!
The paths are aglow with peonies under the fires of immemorial
    colors.
And the breeze from the South troubles the virginal pool with the
whispered secrets of love.

Translated from the French by Dorothy Blair

Flavien Ranaivo (Madagascar)

The Common Lover's Song

Do not love me, cousin,
like a shadow
for shadows vanish with the evening
and I would keep you with me
all night long;
or like pepper
which makes the belly hot
for then I couldn't
satisfy my hunger;
or like a pillow
for then we'd be together
while we're sleeping
but hardly see each other
once it's day;
or like rice
for once swallowed
you think no more of it:
or like sweet words
for they evaporate;
or like honey
sweet enough but all too common.
Love me like a lovely dream,
your life at night,
my hope by day;
like the silver coin
I keep close on earth
and on the great voyage,
a faithful companion;
like a calabash,
intact, for drawing water
in pieces, bridges for my lute.

Old Merina Theme

Plants grow
driven by their roots
and driven by my love I come to you.

At the top of the great trees, my dear,
the bird completes his flight.
My journeys are not done until I'm close to you.

The cascades of Farahantsana tumble, tumble.
They fall, they fall but do not break.

My love for you, my dear,
like water on the sand.
I wait for it to sink, it rises.

Two loves sprang up together
like two twins.
Misfortune to the first who is untrue.

Farewell, my dear, farewell,
careless love may fool the eye,
uncertain love brings madness.

Uncertain love, my dear,
like mist upon the pond.
There's much of it, but not to hold,
for mist upon the pond, my dear,
flirts and then is gone
while avoko flowers
settle 'round the fields.

A chicken snatched by the papango, dear,
and carried high grows lonely
far, far from his love.

Morning memories benumb,
daytime memories tire,
evening memories are delicious,
don't you think, my darling?

The two of us, my dear:
a speck of sand caught in the eye
a tiny thing, but dazing!

The two of us, my dear:
clay accumulating bit by bit
that grows into a house of brick.

Hurry, hurry then
my love,
or night will overtake you.

My limbs will break,
my eyes see dimly,
tell them I can do no more.

Let twilight cover up the earth—
my heart is in eternal moonlight.
Come then to my side.

    They'll scold me at home.
    my elder sister says I mustn't go with you,
    but I don't mind her.

    I love, but can do nothing.
    I love, but am afraid.
    I'll come, but you come with me, dear.

    The door is closed, my dear,
    you come too late, my love,
    they'll scold me.

Open up, I'll tell you secrets—
open up, so we can talk,
open up, I love you!

The door is closed, my darling,
but my heart is open.
so do come in: I love you, cousin.

Is the door not made of reeds, my love,
that you close it with a key?
Open up to me, I'm tired of waiting.

Song of a Young Girl

Oaf
the young man who lives down there
beside the threshing floor for rice;
like two banana-roots
on either side of the village ditch,
we gaze on each other,
we are lovers,
but he won't marry me.
Jealous
his mistress I saw two days since at the wash house
coming down the path against the wind.
She was proud;
was it because she wore a lamba thick
and studded with coral
or because they are newly bedded?
However it isn't the storm
that will flatten the delicate reed,
nor the great sudden shower
at the passage of a cloud
that will startle out of his wits
the blue bull.
I am amazed;
the big sterile rock
survived the rain of the flood
and it's the fire that crackles
the bad grains of maize.
Such this famous smoker
who took tobacco
when there was no more hemp to burn.
A foot of hemp?
—Sprung in Andringitra,
spent in Ankaratra,
no more than cinders to us.
False flattery

stimulates love a little
but the blade has two edges;
why change what is natural?
—If I have made you sad
look at yourself in the water of repentance,
you will decipher there a word I have left.
Good-bye, whirling puzzle,
I give you my blessing:
wrestle with the crocodile,
here are your victuals and three water-lily flowers
for the way is long.

Translated from the French by Gerald Moore

Choice

—Who is she whose-feet-go-clattering-the-hard-ground?
—The daughter of the new chief-of-thousand.
—If it is the daughter of the chief-of-thousand
   tell her soon the night will fall
   and that I will exchange love red as coral
   for a hint of friendship.

—Who is she-who-comes-from-the-north?
—The sister of the widow-with-the-jamerose-perfume.
—Tell her to come in without delay,
   I will prepare her something good to eat.
—She will not taste it, if I know her:
   she takes only rice water
   not because she is thirsty
   but capricious about you.

Distress

—Ohé, long-haired beauty!

—Who goes there?

—I am the one cursed by my father, cursed by
my mother; though small I'm dressed in silk;
though taciturn, my thinking is profound; though
easily chilled I am amber from the sun; being
sensitive, I am sentimental all the more;
a wanderer, though supple is my gait.

—The water cowrie is tiny too, young man;
but many oxen are its victims.
Silent is a glance and yet how eloquent.
As for me I like a bronze skin best,
it gives more warmth.
Nostalgia has a sweetness too
but not from he-who-rubs-his-nose-in-it.
So sink, young man, collapse!
Go founder in your dreams.
Tomorrow's sunrise will be rather late
for I and pining
will be gone
tonight.

The Water-Seeker

A Dove is she
who goes down
the rocky path
sliding like
a capricious pebble
on the steep slope
towards the spring.

The water-seeker.

She descends
with clumsy care,
catching
time and again
with one hand
on the aloe leaves
smooth and pointed,
with the other
she holds the earthen pitcher
—of the country earth—
Scarcely sure
those naked
feet
of the girl of Imerina.
What can she be dreaming
beneath her thick *lamba*
which yet molds
breasts half guessed, sharp
smooth and pointed?
—"What can you be dreaming
Amber-skinned-one
Almond-eyed-one?"—
What can she be thinking
she-who-has-never-known

nor joy nor sorrow
nor love nor hate . . .
Alluring yet
those lying
lips:
so smooth and pointed?
A breath,
the breath of a breeze
has so soon ruffled
her black hair.
What can she be dreaming
this soul-less body
which ruffles
the soul of the poet?
Sweet
deceit.

Translated from the French by Dorothy Blair

Amina

Amina, the choice has fallen on you
   to go,
Like a rose-bud you've shut, after
   you had blossomed,
I pray for you a light leading you
   to heaven.
The love that binds us together,
   none other can unbind.

I longed for your return to health,
   to this end I prayed.
I wish you had not lost, succumbing
   to the ailment,
God's own dictum that it shall be,
   the choice has been yours to go.
The love that binds us together, none
   other can unbind.

My grief is past description, whenever
   I dwell on you,
This and that memory come back, it's
   now but a dream,
I believe not that death betokens the
   end of life.
The love that binds us together,
   none other can unbind.

Imperishable, I believe, is the soul,
   forever will it live,
Death is a salvation, come when it
   comes,
My beloved precious, in Heaven thou
   shalt dwell.

The love that binds us together,
    none other can unbind.

One thing for certain I know and
    remember,
You now dwell, where distress will
    touch you not again,
That is recompense for me left
    now behind.
The love that binds us together,
    none other can unbind.

The poem concludes with a prayer
    to you,
When dust and dust reunite and the
    soul returneth,
And death is no more, love shall be
    reborn,
The love that binds us together,
    none other can unbind.

Remember

It's neither yours nor mine,
    all these are to be shared.
I'm yours, you mine, what's there
    to divide?
Coming together for mortals, that's
    the thing to do,
In God's eyes it is pleasing,
    and so with His angels.
To tell you I am going away,
    that I dare not say,
Neither you my companion, I think not
    that's what you want,
To say "no" is bitter to you, and
    so it is to me.
The world is full of complications,
    that's what I say to you,
    remember.

David Rubadiri (Malawi)

The Witch Tree at Mubende

The Witch Tree
old and knobbly
stood with years
scratched by a cross
abused
as cameras clicked
and learned tongues discoursed.

Naked it stood
in its age of mysteries.

Beauty and innocence
stood there too
side by side—
two witches
as I saw them
prismatic lenses prying
the old and the new—

To me she was then
the Mubende Witch Tree.

An African Vigil

Evening drapes gold on distant hills
as slowly along the winding footpath
I walk to meet her
my dark lady.

She will be at the waterhole
drawing the day's last pot of water.
As I turn round these familiar bushes
my heart knows she will be there
as it has been
since first we kept vigil.

I stand and wait—
First appears her pot
then bare brown shoulders
a slender neck
fringed with round beads
of a fiery sunset glow,
a slow turn of dark eyes
a lightning shadow of a smile—

That is all she ever says
that is all I wish to hear.
She steps aside to let me pass.
As I edge my way past her,
her eyes meet my eyes
     for a moment
      that lingers timelessly
      dwelling on each other understandingly

Same time tomorrow? my eyes say,
hers: I shall not fail.

The Prostitute

I desired her
truly, like all men
in the dark cascades
of the Suzana desire beautiful
and seductive women;
the Congo beat
rippled through her
shimmering
along a bottom
down to her feet.

The morning of the night
burst through my thighs
in a longing of fire—
she
almost a goddess
lit
in clever cascades
of light.
But in the light of another morning,
after the jingle of pennies,
how could I move
to stir the glue-pot?

Tijan M. Sallah (Gambia)

Love

I have often loved you, you
With the sweet grace of a giraffe.
My heart's room gathers warmth
From your firewood-presence.
You have been my pillar;
Erect stem to lean my trust.
You have been my *bentenki* tree,
And I, the elephant, leaning
On your back.

But now it seems
You feed on my blemishes.
You see, love needs a new skin,
A new talk. Otherwise, love finds
Comfort in petty faults.

You stand now under the sun;
Your eyes collect nightmares
From the sight of me.
You grin the mixed smile
Of a hyena. You smile,
When you mean the opposite.
You laugh, when you mean
A spear should be thrust
Into my heart.

But you still remind me
Of those days in Brikama,*
When you were a young girl
With some dandruff in your hair,
Those days when you were you,
Not some magazine photo model;

When success had not carved
A musky pride in your head.

You see, it seems
Time trims the genuine
Out of love
If the two bean-lobes
Of love
Are not careful.

You stand there, sullen
As the sky before a rain.
Root of my heart, I want you
To rain happiness
And drift to that old earth
Where the old self dwells
In the naked love of giraffes.

I want you to wear those waist beads
And move with the tender waist-shake
Of a *laubeh*.** I want you to come,
Perfuming the air with *gonga*.

For I do not care
How much money you make now,
Or the type of prestige-car you drive;
Our love has never been
About benzes or jaguars.
I do not care about
How many cities you travel to,
Or men you put in their place;
Our love has never been
About your success against mine.

All I know is that
Our love has been about love,

The sweet, earth-goddess love
Of tubers. And about
Our children and
The seeds they should gather
To plant trees of the future.

And if things should intervene,
They should only be treated as things.
And love should still be love,
And make-ups still make-ups,
Before we lose ourselves
In this mad harvest of city lights.

* Brikama: a town situated about sixteen miles from Banjul, Gambia.
** *laubeh*: a member of the lower caste of the Fulani ethnic group found in Senegal and Gambia known for their seductiveness and sexual prowess.

Woman

for F. Haidara

You have my unqualified love.
Flowers lean on the slender waist
Of your door knob. This is no
Hoary love; no love to toss
In the waste-basket.

I see you in my mirror every day,
Love images in plenitude.
You extend your lips
In syllables of charm;
I extend mine. Like elephants,
We fuse our proboscises
In the amorous moonlight.

Woman, there is nothing
On this garrulous earth;
Nothing, not even garlands
On the feet of sacred stone circles
That match your grace.

The way you walk, terraces of flower-shades.
Each step practised to the
Rhythm of the imaginary drum.
Each waist-shake, each hand movement,
Like the flawless gestures of a ballet-dancer.

Woman, tall beauty of giraffe-grace,
Like the slender palm trees of Jeswang,*
Like the ostrich I saw at Niokoloba.
You compete with the beams of sun and moon.
And you trap shades of beauty
Under your armpit.

Woman, you are Timbuktu.
Salt rides every part of your aura.
You nibble books like fish do plankton.
You anchor your head
On the rock of tradition.

You are beauty, clothed in kindness.
Your days are filled with *terranga*.**
Woman, you are the nectar that perfumes my seasons.
And I stand here today like a bard-flower,
Your beauty overwhelming my savage days.

* Jeswang: a town between Banjul and Serre Kunda, Gambia.
** *terranga*: Senegambian hospitality.

Léopold Sédar Senghor (Senegal)

You Held the Black Face

[for Khalam]

You held the black face of the warrior between your hands
Which seemed with fateful twilight luminous.
From the hill I watched the sunset in the bays of your eyes.
When shall I see my land again, the pure horizon of your face?
When shall I sit at the table of your dark breasts?
The nest of sweet decisions lies in the shade.
I shall see different skies and different eyes,
And shall drink from the sources of other lips, fresher than lemons,
I shall sleep under the roofs of other hair, protected from storms.
But every year, when the rum of spring kindles the veins afresh,
I shall mourn anew my home, and the rain of your eyes over the
    thirsty savannah.

Translated from the French by Gerald Moore and Ulli Beier

I Will Pronounce Your Name

[for Tama]

I will pronounce your name, Naëtt, I will declaim you, Naëtt!
Naëtt, your name is mild like cinnamon, it is the fragrance in which
    the lemon grove sleeps,
Naëtt, your name is the sugared clarity of blooming coffee trees
And it resembles the savannah, that blossoms forth under the
    masculine ardor of the midday sun.
Name of dew, fresher than shadows of tamarind,
Fresher even than the short dusk, when the heat of the day is
    silenced.
Naëtt, that is the dry tornado, the hard clap of lightning
Naëtt, coin of gold, shining coal, you my night, my sun! . . .
I am your hero, and now I have become your sorcerer, in order to
    pronounce your names.
Princess of Elissa, banished from the Futa on that fateful day.

Translated from the French by Gerald Moore and Ulli Beier

I Have Spun a Song Soft

[for Two Flutes]

I have spun a song soft as a murmur of doves at
    noon
To the shrill notes of my four-string khalam.
I have woven you a song and you did not hear me.
I have offered you wild flowers with scents as strange
    as a sorcerer's eyes
I have offered you my wild flowers. Will you let
    them wither,
Finding distraction in the mayflies dancing?

Translated from the French by John Reed and Clive Wake

A Hand of Light Caressed My Eyelids

[for flutes]

A hand of light has caressed my eyelids of darkness
And your smile rose like the sun on the mists drifting grey
    and cold over my Congo.
My heart has echoed the virgin song of the
    dawn-birds
As my blood kept time once to the white song of the
    sap in the branches of my arms.
See, the bush flower and the star in my hair, and the band
    round the forehead of the herdsman athlete.
I will take the flute, I will make a rhythm for the slow peace
    of the herds
And all day sitting in the shade of your eyelashes, close to the
    Fountain of Fimla,
I shall faithfully pasture the flaxen lowings of your herds,
For this morning a hand of light caressed my eyelids of darkness
And all day long my heart has echoed the virgin song of the
    birds.

Translated from the French by John Reed and Clive Wake

Was It a Mograbin Night?

[for two flutes and a distant drum]

Was it a Mograbin night? I leave Mogador with its platinum
    daughters.
Was it a Mograbin night? It was also the Night our night of
    Joal
Before we were born, inexpressible night: you did up your hair
    in the mirror of my eyes.

We sat anxiously in the shadow of our secret
Anxiously waiting and your nostrils quivered.
Do you remember that noise of peace? from the lower town,
    wave upon wave
Till it was breaking at our feet. In the distance a lighthouse
    called to my right
To my left, next to my heart, the strange immobility of your
    eyes.
These sudden flashes of lightning in the night of the rainy
    season—I could read your face
And I took long parched draughts of your terrible face and
    they inflamed my thirst
And in my astonished heart in my heart of silence in my
    nonplussed heart
Those gusts of barking down there that burst it like a grenade.
Then the bronze crunch of sand, the leaves flickered like eyelids.
The black guards passed by, giant gods of Eden: moon-faced
    moths
Rested gently on their arms—their happiness scalded us.

Listening to our hearts, we heard them beating down there at
    Fadioutt
We heard the earth tremble under the conquering feet of the
    athletes

And the voice of the Beloved singing the shadowy splendor
    of the Lover.
And we dared not move our trembling hands, and our mouths
    opened and closed.
And if the eagle suddenly flung itself at our breast, with a
    comet's fierce cry?
But the irresistible current carried me away towards the
    horrible song of the reefs of your eyes.

There will be other nights my dear. You will come again to sit
    in this bank of shadow
You will always be the same and you will not be the same.
Does it matter? Through all your transformations, I shall
    worship the features of Koumba Tam.

Translated from the French by John Reed and Clive Wake

I Came with You as Far as the Village

[for Khalam]

I came with you as far as the village of grain-huts, to the gates
    of Night
I had no words before the golden riddle of your smile.
A brief twilight fell on your face, freak of the divine fancy.
From the top of the hill where the light takes refuge, I saw the
    brightness of your cloth go out
And your crest like a sun dropped beneath the shadow of the
    ricefields
When anxieties came against me, ancestral fears
    more treacherous than panthers
—The mind cannot push them back across the day's horizons.
Is it then night for ever, parting never to meet again?
I shall weep in the darkness, in the motherly hollow of the Earth
I will sleep in the silence of my tears
Until my forehead is touched by the milky dawning of your
    mouth.

Translated from the French by John Reed and Clive Wake

Abdul Hakim Mahmoud El-Sheikh (Eritrea)

Breaths of Saffron on Broken Mirrors

Lust won't leave me alone
Confused and wanting you
Bathed in juicy colors
As we fall on each other
And I bathe like a hero
In your body full of desire . . .
But it's me hissing
And a little water
Before I'm feeling guilty
Until I see these notes
Echoing outside and not unnatural
But as joy with passion
And turning me upside down,
Oblivious to any niceties
Of the thin water of reason.
I remember love again,
A time to write poetry
Without carving it on my forehead,
When I shun both sides of the river
To look in the mirror of its flowing.
I see love born amidst three stories:
Oleander covering my face;
Writing I see on the feet
Of some poor farmers walking by;
And how the peace we found in trees
Filled us so deeply
That we discovered the power of revolution.
Can you imagine my fascination
When birdsong attacked a meadow
That bloomed only for my eyes
Before my own tongue took over
Prophesying a newborn amidst the sheaves

Of wheat in the gleam of harvest?
And why this chant sulking in the cypress
Before tumbling through the branches
And overpowering a man
Known as a lily in the field?
Like henna lines we surrounded him
Before a dream vision
Of strong language like radiation
Repelling love in action
Required a heart-to-heart conversation.
Before I was so angry
I was smoother than a lentil
And full of nurture overflowing
For a thousand wounded,
Another thousand dead,
And one particular woman
Passing away forever to that far shore
Between my wanting and leaving her.
Listen. From now on,
Never will I waste another day,
Never, even if I have no poetry,
Even if I reject every single word,
Never again will I waste a single day—
At least not as long as I love
To see her smile so clearly
And find her body's wild curves
In the waves crashing to shore
For a song of our martyrs' remains.

Translated from the Arabic by Charles Cantalupo and Ghirmai Negash

Abeba

Abeba, my flower from Asmara . . .

Measured and subtle
As her makeup
And her finely drawn eyes—
She spoke like poetry.

The food her family sent
To prison everyday
Arrived as usual
The day her grave was dug.
I heard her cry.

Later that night I also heard
The prison guard
Summon her out
And the shot.

She lives in my dreams
And refuses to leave,
Knowing all my secrets
And never letting me rest.

Before she died
She wove a basket
Inscribed "for my parents"

Abeba, my flower from Asmara . . .
Who never blossomed.
My cell-mate.

Translated from Tigrinya by Charles Cantalupo and Ghirmai Negash

Adam Small (South Africa)

What abou' de Lô?

Diana was a white girl
Martin was a black boy

they fell in love
they fell in love
they fell in love

Said Diana's folks
What abou' de Lô
Said Martin's folks
What abou' de Lô
said everyone's folks
What abou' de Lô

Said Diana, said Martin
What Lô?
God's Lô
man's Lô
devil's Lô
what Lô

But the folks just said
de Lô
de Lô
de Lô
de Lô
what abou' de Lô
what abou' de Lô

Diana was a white girl
Martin was a black boy

they go to jail
they go to jail
they go to jail

Said Diana's folks
See, we told you mos
Said Martin's folks
See, we told you mos
said everyone's folks
see, we told you mos

Said Diana, said Martin
what you tell
what God tell
what man tell
what devil tell
what you tell?

But the folks just said
de Lô
de Lô
de Lô
de Lô
what abou' de Lô, huh
what abou' de Lô?

Diana was a white girl
Martin was a black boy

Diana commit suicide
Martin commit suicide
Diana and Martin commit suicide

Say Diana's folks
O God protect
Say Martin's folks

O God protect
Say everyone's folks
O God protect

Diana and Martin they died for de Lô
God's Lô
man's Lô
devil's Lô
what Lô?

And the folks just said
de Lô
de Lô
de Lô
de Lô
What abou' de Lô
What abou' de Lô?

Benedict W. Vilakazi (South Africa)

Umamina

Come Mamina,
Come let us stretch our legs and thither go,
There where it is wilderness
There where water fountains spring
Dampening the deep green rocks,
Slippery with slimy moss.

Nay Mamina,
Come out as though to draw water,
Carry a calabash and descend to the river.
There you will find me under the water-myrtle
Heavy in full bloom,
Black and oozing with thick juice.

Come Mamina,
Alone, you are bright with crimson hue,
Your path adorned with gaudy colors,
Blossoming with flowers,
Which stoop before you
Bowing their heads on the earth.

Come Mamina,
When you did gaze on me, ebony maiden,
I knew not whither I would go,
My knees quivered, my weapons dropped,
I was filled with the bitterness that lurks in the heart
Like a wild beast, and is called love.

Alas, I seek you, Mamina,
You have hidden in the fields of dry grass.
The dry grass is my soul,
Yet you are loitering there,
Gathering blackberries, herbs and creepers.

It is not the national song of shields and knobkerries I sing.
In truth I chant in harmony with the music of your reed-pipe,
Whose tunes I hear in the land of Chaka.
I heard and listened and knew.
I beheld your dark complexioned lips
Close over the singing reed-pipe,
Which recalls the golden-rumped canary of the forest.
I would that it were blown by the heart
Which harbors thought and feeling.
You have made me grow thus with love,
That I no more appear as a Zulu
Within the courtyard of the black people.

Your love and mine, O Mamina,
Excel the mind, beyond the power of the diviners,
Whose magic bones are strewn on the ground.
They grind herbs and poisonous bushes.
"In truth, are you not deceiving me, Mamina?"
I ask you, as I gaze into
The center of your eyes without blinking:
"Are you not one of the ancestral spirits?"
Perchance you have lost your way,
On your journey to the gates of Heaven,
And have branched off to Earth,
And chanced on the roots of love.

Come Mamina,
You are the star of my soul
You alone are in the depth of my veins
Which make my heart tremble.
You are like the track of the field rat
Which winds through old grass and heads far off.

Come Mamina,
I feel loneliness steal over me.
This earth affords no refuge for me.

Come and lead me to your land, Mamina.
There let us solve the mystery of this love,
That I may know it, Mamina;
Know it wholly with the spirit of the ancestors.

Translated from the Zulu by R. M. Mfeka and adapted by Peggy Rutherford

Patricia Jabbeh Wesley (Liberia)

Nyanken Hne

My husband, Nyanken Hne,
like *galo*, waving up Dolokeh's hills.
The storms cannot touch him;
they fear him like a wife fears a jealous man.
The young girls with their shining eyes,
whose lashes wave, stand off the road
when Nyanken Hne passes.
Their pails of water fall off their heads
to see Nyanken Hne pass by.

My husband, Nyanken Hne,
who came amidst polished smiles, long,
dark, chalked faces, bowing when he passes.
Nyanken came, dancing my way,
in a war dance, shining like ebony.
How I love to look at him dancing
to giant drums beating in the dusky wind.
How Nyanken passed them all by
while they called him with swinging
oiled, brown arms, dancing.
But Nyanken chose only me.

Nyanken has said I am the only one.
He has broken taboos, has shattered
their good dreams.
All these years, Nyanken has said, no,
I am the only one.
When I rise, Nyanken is there,
like the mighty, rising *Sebo*.
Unlike our townsmen whose eyes
never quit hunting, Nyanken has only me.
When I sit, he looks down into my eyes,
and they all stand and stare.

Surrender

So often, I want to make you;
roll you, reshape you, a ball of clay
after my say.
I want to squeeze you,
my play dough, an image,
into my image.
I want to melt you, shape you, like gold;
polish you, mold you into a charm
to be sold.

My little woodwork, carve you,
make you my *Kissi* ritual mask.
I want to hang you
so often, around these, my walls,
make you my little talisman,
swing you, my little magic wand.

My pungent, leafy *voodoo*,
my *sumu*, my boiling pot of *juju*.
My little protective pin
about my fabric life, about my pieces.
I want to ride you, my cruising Pajaro.
Suddenly, there
you are, always God.

Now, it is your turn. Here, roll me,
reshape me, pat me, mold me,
heating the clay of my flesh,
after your flesh.

Grip hold of my mascara cheeks, my charms
of gold bracelets, binding my life.
Melt all my magic wands,
my bulging, voodoo eyes.

Take hold of my big, bleeding heart,
my boiling pot of *juju*, my beads
of charms, my me.
And if I'm not yet surrendered,
my God, vanquish me.

Dan Wylie (Zimbabwe/South Africa)

Loving This Younger Woman

is like holding in the palm
a pearl of inscrutable price, a moon
of impenetrable charm.

My whetstone, my bright
onyx! When will she strike fire
out of this demure light?

I long for pride, or anger,
for the violence of trust, a more
than ordinary hunger:

like the moon, she is so
mannered, angelic in her taught
orbit, her magnesium glow

in independent space
presenting to this flinty earth
the one unblemished face.

And even as my hands ape
a reconstructed youth, and reach
to touch her shadowed nape,

a gravity intervenes,
her brilliant innocence gulfs
again outdistancing the dreams.

Loving This Older Woman

is like walking on the thin
surface of the moon, the skull
too close beneath the skin.

Why do I so youthfully embrace
death, kiss the seismic troubles
that have mapped her face,

courting its reliable eclipse?
Her breasts fill my palms like gourds
of forming cheese, her lips

carouse and part, obedient
to suggestion as a girl's. But
there's the end, apparent

as a birthmark, etched
in acid, the pocked and empty sea,
unflinching as a ghost.

She is so luminous and worn,
her dusty smile, tough wisdom, hope,
and the flesh loosened on the bone.

No use pretending to mark
time: time wrinkles at the wrist,
the moon's lid shuts in the dark.

Ending It

It is too early to be sitting outside.
The garden is blue with dissolution.

But we sit here, in glacial air, until
her glance throws scalding loops around my shoulders.

 "Can't you at least *try* to explain?" she
manages to say; I cannot bring myself

to answer, *You are not the woman with whom
I wish to grow old.* I hug my withdrawal

to my chest like a punctured ball.
"This doesn't make either of us bad," I demur.

Silence, heavy as benches. In time, it lightens,
doves whinny, we almost laugh at the quizzical hens.

At last: "The dew is so beautiful." Dewdrops
on her cheeks, falling faster than stars.

And: "I wonder where *he's* going": an ant,
hefting his penance through tremendous grass.

Simultaneously, separately, gratefully, we
lift our faces to the warmth of the permanent sun.

Credits
Contributors

Credits

Grateful acknowledgment is hereby extended to the following publishers and poets for permission to publish or reprint their work in this anthology:

Ancient Egyptian: "My Love Is Back, Let Me Shout Out the News," "If I Could Just Be the Washerman," "I Cannot Condone, My Heart, Your Loving," "Love, How I'd Love to Slip Down to the Pond," "Palm Trees, Heavy with Dates," "If Ever, My Dear One, I Should Not Be Here," "My Love Is One and Only, Without Peer," and "Flee Him, My Heart—and Hurry," are reprinted from *Love Songs of the New Kingdom*, translated by John L. Foster, Copyright © 1969, 1970, 1972, 1973, 1974. Used by permission of the University of Texas Press. "For a Portrait of the Queen" and "Spell for Causing the Beloved to Follow After" are reprinted from *Ancient Egyptian Literature: An Anthology*, translated by John L. Foster, Copyright © 2001. Used by permission of the University of Texas Press.

Aandonga: "Love Praise" and "Song of a Bridegroom in Praise of His Bride" are reprinted from Willard R. Trask, ed., *The Unwritten Song: Poetry of the Primitive and Traditional Peoples of the World*, vol. 1, *The Far North, Africa, Indonesia, Melanesia, Australia* (New York: Macmillan Co., 1966).

Acoli: "Lightning, Strike My Husband," "Where Has My Love Blown His Horn?," and "When I See the Beauty on My Beloved's Face" are reprinted from Okot p'Bitek, *Horn of My Love* (London: Heinemann, 1974). Used by permission of Pearson Education.

Akan: "Love Songs" is reprinted from Leonard W. Doob, ed., *Ants Will Not Eat Your Fingers: A Selection of Traditional African Poems* (New York: Walker and Co., 1966). Used by permission of Walker and Co.

Bagirmi: "Love Song" is reprinted from Ulli Beier, ed., *African Poetry: An Anthology of Traditional African Poems* (New York: Cambridge University Press, 1966).

Bambara: "Love Defeats Queen Saran" is excerpted and reprinted from Hampate Bâ, *Monzon et le roi de Koré*, *Présence Africaine*, No. 58, 2e Trimestre, Paris, 1966. Used by permission of Jacques-Noël Gouat, translator.

Baule: "Women's Song" is from Maurice Delafosse, *Essai de manuel de langue agni parlée dans la moitié orientale de la Côte d'Ivoire* (Paris: Librarie Africaine et Coloniale, 1900). Reprinted from Willard R. Trask, ed., *The Unwritten Song: Poetry of the Primitive and Traditional Peoples of the World*, vol. 1, *The Far North, Africa, Indonesia, Melanesia, Australia* (New York: Macmillan Co., 1966).

Berber: "I Want to Be with My Love in a Garden," "I Want to Be in a Garden with My Love," and "My Passion Is Like Turbulence at the Head of Waters" are reprinted from Aliki Barnstone and Willis Barnstone, eds., *A Book of Women Poets from Antiquity to Now* (New York: Schocken Books, 1980). Used by permission of Willis Barnstone, translator. "Love Songs" is from M. Abès, "Monographie d'une tribu berbère: Les Aïth Ndhir (Beni M'tir)," *Archives Berbères* 3 (1918). Reprinted from Willard R. Trask, ed., *The Unwritten Song: Poetry of the Primitive and Traditional Peoples of the World*, vol. 1, *The Far North, Africa, Indonesia, Melanesia, Australia* (New York: Macmillan Co., 1966).

Didinga or Lango: "A Mother to Her First-Born" is from Jack Herbert Driberg, *Initiation: Translations from Poems of the Didinga and Lango Tribes* (Great Britain: Golden Cockrel Press, 1932). Reprinted from Willard R. Trask, ed., *The Unwritten Song: Poetry of the Primitive and Traditional Peoples of the World*, vol. 1, *The Far North, Africa, Indonesia, Melanesia, Australia* (New York: Macmillan Co., 1966).

Dogon: "Encouraging a Dancer" is reprinted from Willard R. Trask, ed., *Classic Black African Poems* (New York: Earkins Press, 1971). Used by permission of the Earkins Press.

Kipsigi: "Girls' Secret Love Song" is reprinted from Leonard W. Doob, ed., *Ants Will Not Eat Your Fingers: A Selection of Traditional African Poems* (New York: Walker and Co., 1966). Used by permission of Walker and Co.

Merina: "Dialogues" and "Girls' Songs" are from Jean Laulhan, *Les Hain-teny merinas, poésies populaires malgaches* (Paris: Librarie Paul Geuthner, 1913). Reprinted from Willard R. Trask, ed., *The Unwritten Song: Poetry of the Primitive* and *Traditional Peoples of the World*, vol. 1, *The Far North, Africa, Indonesia, Melanesia, Australia* (New York: Macmillan Co., 1966).

Swahili: "Love Does Not Know Secrets," "Love," and "A Match in Petrol" are reprinted from Jan Knappert, ed., *An Anthology of Swahili Love Poetry* (Berkeley: University of California Press, 1972). "In Praise of Love" is reprinted from Jan Knappert, ed., *Four Centuries of Swahili Verse: A Literary History and Anthology* (London: Heinemann, 1979).

Teda: "To Fatima" is reprinted from Leonard W. Doob, ed., *Ants Will Not Eat Your Fingers: A Selection of Traditional African Poems* (New York: Walker and Co., 1966). Used by permission of Walker and Co.

Thonga: "Complaint of a Jilted Lover" is reprinted from Leonard W. Doob, ed., *Ants Will Not Eat Your Fingers: A Selection of Traditional African Poems* (New York: Walker and Co., 1966). Used by permission of Walker and Co.

Tuareg: "Girl's Song" and "In Praise of Abazza Ag Mekiia" are from Charles Eugène de Foucauld, *Poésies touarègues—Dialecte de l'Ähaggar,* edited by André Basset, 2 vols. (Paris: Ernest Leroux, 1925–30). Reprinted from Willard R. Trask, ed., *The Unwritten Song: Poetry of the Primitive and Traditional Peoples of the World*, vol. 1, *The Far North, Africa, Indonesia, Melanesia, Australia* (New York: Macmillan Co., 1966).

Xhosa: "Love Song of a Girl" is reprinted from Leonard W. Doob, ed., *Ants Will Not Eat Your Fingers: A Selection of Traditional African Poems* (New York: Walker and Co., 1966). Used by permission of Walker and Co.

Zulu: "Zulu Love Song" is reprinted from Charlotte and Wold Leslau, eds., *African Poems and Love Songs* (Mount Vernon, N.Y.: Peter Pauper Press, 1970). Used by permission of the publisher.

Abderrahim Afarki: "A Good Day to You, Si Mohammad" appears courtesy of the author. Used by permission of Jacques-Noël Gouat, translator.

Mririda n'Aït Attik: "The Bad Lover," "What Do You Want?," "Azouou," "Azouou's Reply," and "The Brooch" are reprinted from Daniel Halpern and Paula Paley, trans., *The Songs of Mririda, Courtesan of the High Atlas* (Greensboro, N.C.: Unicorn Press, 1974). Used by permission of Daniel Halpern.

Lounis Aït-Menguellet: "Love, Love, Love" and "It Was Like a Nightmare" are reprinted from *The Literary Review,* vol. 41, no. 2 (Winter 1998). Used by permission of Rabah Seffal, translator.

Ifi Amadiume: "Show Me All," "One Kiss," "Dubem's Patience," "A Passing Feeling," and "Gypsy Woman" are reprinted from *Ecstasy* (Lagos, Nigeria: Longman Nigeria, 1995). Used by permission of the author.

Kofi Awoonor: "The New Warmth" is from *Night of My Blood* (New York: Doubleday, 1971); "Lover's Song" and "Lovers' Song" are from *Rediscovery* (Ibadan: Mbari Publications, 1964). Used by permission of the author.

Gabeba Baderoon: "Beginning," "Finding You," "Where Nothing Was," and "The Dream in the Next Body" are reprinted from *The Dream in the Next*

Body (Cape Town: Kwela Books/Snailpress, 2005). Used by permission of the author.

Juma Bhalo: "The Eyes or the Heart?," "A Certain Person," and "My Beloved" are reprinted from Lyndon Harries, trans. and ed., *Poems from Kenya: Gnomic Verses in Swahili by Ahmad Nassir bin Juma Bhalo* (Madison: University of Wisconsin Press, 1966). Used by permission of University of Wisconsin Press. "The Love of Which I Speak" is reprinted from Jan Knappert, ed., *Four Centuries of Swahili Verse: A Literary History and Anthology* (London: Heinemann, 1979).

Syl Cheney-Coker: "To My Wife Dying of Cancer (1)," "To My Wife Dying of Cancer (2)," and "Homecoming" appear here for the first time. "Poem for a Lost Lover" is reprinted from *The Graveyard Also Has Teeth* (Oxford: Heinemann, 1980). Used by permission of the author.

Frank M. Chipasula: "Chipo::Gift," "Hands That Give," "The Kiss," and "Wife/Life" © Frank M. Chipasula. "A Song in Spring" is reprinted from Elizabeth Bartlett, ed., *Literary Olympians* (Boston: Ford-Brown and Co., 1992).

Siriman Cissoko: "O Tulip, Tulip I Have Chosen" is reprinted from *Ressac de nous-mêmes: poèmes* (Paris: Présence Africaine, 1969). Used by permission of Présence Africaine.

José Craveirinha: "Just" first appeared in *Bashiru* (University of Wisconsin–Madison). Used by permission of Arthur Brakel, translator.

David Diop: "Rama Kam," "Close to You," and "To My Mother" are reprinted from *Hammerblows and Other Writings* (Bloomington: Indiana University Press, 1973). Used by permission of Indiana University Press.

Isobel Dixon: "Love Is a Shadow," "Aftertaste," "You, Me and the Orang-utan," "Cusp of Venus," "Intimacy," and "Giving Blood" are from Isobel Dixon. Used by permission of the author.

Emanuel Dongala: "Fantasy under the Moon" is reprinted from Gerald Moore and Ulli Beier, eds., *The Penguin Book of Modern African Poetry* (London: Penguin Books, 1998). Used by permission of the author.

Reesom Haile: "Love in the Daytime," "'I Love You' II," "Ferenji and Habesha," "Whose Daughter?," and "Talking about Love" are reprinted from *We Have Our Voice: Selected Poems of Reesom Haile* (Trenton, N.J.: Red Sea Press, 2000). Used by permission of Africa World Press.

Beyene Hailemariam: "Silas" and "Let's Divorce and Get Married Again" are reprinted from Charles Cantalupo and Ghirmai Negash, eds., *Who Needs a Story? Contemporary Eritrean Poetry in Tigrinya, Tigre and Arabic* (Asmara, Eritrea: Hdri Publishers, 2005). Used by permission of Hdri Publishers.

Naana Banyiwa Horne: "Sounding Drum," "You Rock My World," "*Sore Ka Pra*: Whoopie, Akan Time," and "Happy Father's Day" are reprinted from *Sunkwa: Clingings onto Life* (Trenton, N.J.: Africa World Press, 1999). Used by permission of Africa World Press.

Ahmad Basheikh Husein: "Messenger, I Send You," "Love Is Not Sweet," and "I Have No More to Say: Love Is Finished" are reprinted from Jan Knappert, ed., *Four Centuries of Swahili Verse: A Literary History and Anthology* (London: Heinemann, 1979).

Rashidah Ismaili: "Clandestine," "Confessions," "*Chez toi*," and "Alone" are reprinted from *Missing in Action and Presumed Dead* (Trenton, N.J.: Africa World Press, 1992). Used by permission of the author.

António Jacinto: "Love Poem" is reprinted from Margaret Dickinson, ed., *When Bullets Begin to Flower* (Nairobi: East African Publishing House, 1972). Used by permission of East African Educational Publishers. "Letter from a Contract Worker" is reprinted from Frank M. Chipasula, ed., *When My Brothers Come Home: Poems from Central and Southern Africa* (Middletown, Conn.: Wesleyan University Press, 1985). Used by permission of Wesleyan University Press.

David Kerr: "Elemental" and "Swimming Pool Sacrament" are reprinted from *Tangled Tongues* (Hexham, U.K.: Flambard, 2003). "The Tattoo" was first published in *Pulsar Poetry Magazine* 13 (1998). "Wet and Dry" appears here for the first time. Used by permission of the author.

Saba Kidane: "Go Crazy Over Me" is reprinted from Charles Cantalupo and Ghirmai Negash, eds., *Who Needs a Story? Contemporary Eritrean Poetry in Tigrinya, Tigre and Arabic* (Asmara, Eritrea: Hdri Publishers, 2005). Used by permission of Hdri Publishers.

Daniel P. Kunene: "Will You, My Dark-Brown Sister?," "Music of the Violin," "It Is Not the Clouds," and "Red" are used by permission of the author.

Liyongo Fumo: "The Adventure in the Garden," "Ode to Mwana Munga," and "The Song of the Lotus Tree" are reprinted from Jan Knappert, ed., *Four Centuries of Swahili Verse: A Literary History and Anthology* (London: Heinemann, 1979).

Lindiwe Mabuza: "A Love Song" and "Another Song of Love" are reprinted from *Letter to Letta* (Braamfontein, Johannesburg: Skotaville Publishers, 1991). "Shanghai Suite," "Jacarandas for Love," and "Long-Distance Love" appear here for the first time. Used by permission of the author.

Kristina Masuwa-Morgan: "This Morning," "Farewell Love," "Timeless Love," and "We Part . . ." are reprinted from Kristina Rungano, *A Storm Is Brewing* (Harare: Zimbabwe Publishing House, 1984). Used by permission of the author.

Makhokolotso K. A. Mokhomo: "When He Spoke to Me of Love" is reprinted from Jack Cope and Uys Krige, eds., *The Penguin Book of South African Verse* (London: Penguin Books, 1968).

Lupenga Mphande: "Maria's Photograph," "Search for a Bride," and "The Feet of a Dancer" are reprinted from *A Crackle at Midnight* (Lagos, Nigeria: Heinemann Educational Books, 1998). Used by permission of the author.

Muyaka bin Haji: "A Poem to His First Wife," "When We Shall Meet, You and I!," and "The Shawl" are reprinted from Jan Knappert, ed., *Four Centuries of Swahili Verse: A Literary History and Anthology* (London: Heinemann, 1979).

Mvula ya Nangolo: "In the Village" is reprinted from *Watering the Beloved Desert* (Makanda, Ill.: Brown Turtle Press, 2008). "Desert Sandwich" is reprinted from *Thoughts from Exile* (Windhoek, Namibia: Longman Namibia, 1991). Used by permission of the author.

António Agostinho Neto: "A Bouquet of Roses for You" and "Two Years Away" are reprinted from *Sacred Hope* (Dar es Salaam, Tanzania: Tanzania Publishing House, 1974). Used by permission of Marga Holness.

Gabriel Okara: "Silent Girl," "To Paveba," "To a Star," and "Celestial Song" are reprinted from *The Fisherman's Invocation* (Oxford: Heinemann, 1978). Used by permission of the author.

Mohammed Said Osman: "Juket" is reprinted from Charles Cantalupo and Ghirmai Negash, eds., *Who Needs a Story? Contemporary Eritrean Poetry in Tigrinya, Tigre and Arabic* (Asmara, Eritrea: Hdri Publishers, 2005). Used by permission of Hdri Publishers.

Niyi Osundare: "Words Catch Fire" is reprinted from *The Word Is an Egg* (Lagos, Nigeria: Kraft Books, 2000). "Puzzle," "Divine Command," "You Are," "Love in a Season of Terror," and "Tender Moment" are reprinted from *Tender Moments* (Lagos, Nigeria: University Press PLC, 2006). Used by permission of the author.

Jean-Joseph Rabéarivelo: "There You Are" and excerpts from *Old Songs of Imerina Land* are reprinted from Ellen Conroy Kennedy, ed., *The Negritude Poets: An Anthology of Translations from the French* (New York: Thunder's Mouth Press, 1975). Used by permission of Ellen Conroy Kennedy.

Jacques Rabémananjara: "The Lyre with Seven Strings" is reprinted from Peggy Rutherford, ed., *African Voices: An Anthology of Native African Writing* (New York: Vanguard Press, 1960).

Flavien Ranaivo: "The Common Lover's Song," "Old Merina Theme," "Choice," and "Distress" are reprinted from Ellen Conroy Kennedy, ed., *The Negritude Poets: An Anthology of Translations from the French* (New York: Thunder's Mouth Press, 1975). Used by permission of Ellen Conroy Kennedy. "Song of a Young Girl" is reprinted from Gerald Moore and Ulli Beier, eds., *The Penguin Book of Modern African Poetry* (London: Penguin Books, 1998). Used by permission of Gerald Moore, translator. "The Water-Seeker" is reprinted from Peggy Rutherford, ed., *African Voices: An Anthology of Native African Writing* (New York: Vanguard Press, 1960).

Shaaban Robert: "Amina" and "Remember" are reprinted from Ali A. Jahadhmy, ed., *Anthology of Swahili Poetry* (London: Heinemann, 1977). Used by permission of East African Educational Publishers.

David Rubadiri: "The Witch Tree at Mubende," "An African Vigil," and "The Prostitute" are reprinted from *An African Thunderstorm and Other Poems*

(Nairobi: East African Educational Publishers, 2004). Used by permission of the author.

Tijan M. Sallah: "Love" and "Woman" are reprinted from *Dreams of Dusty Roads* (Washington, D.C.: Three Continents Press, 1993). Used by permission of the author.

Léopold Sédar Senghor: "You Held the Black Face" and "I Will Pronounce Your Name" are reprinted from Gerald Moore and Ulli Beier, eds., *The Penguin Book of Modern African Poetry* (London: Penguin Books, 1998). Used by permission of Gerald Moore. "I Have Spun a Song Soft," "A Hand of Light Caressed My Eyelids," "Was It a Mograbin Night?," and "I Came with You as Far as the Village" are reprinted from *Nocturnes,* translated by John Reed and Clive Wake (1961; New York: Third Press, Joseph Okpaku Publishing Company, Inc., 1971).

Abdul Hakim Mahmoud El-Sheikh: "Breaths of Saffron on Broken Mirrors" is reprinted from Charles Cantalupo and Ghirmai Negash, eds., *Who Needs a Story? Contemporary Eritrean Poetry in Tigrinya, Tigre and Arabic* (Asmara, Eritrea: Hdri Publishers, 2005). Used by permission of Hdri Publishers.

Ribka Sibhatu: "Abeba" is reprinted from Charles Cantalupo and Ghirmai Negash, eds., *Who Needs a Story? Contemporary Eritrean Poetry in Tigrinya, Tigre and Arabic* (Asmara, Eritrea: Hdri Publishers, 2005). Used by permission of Hdri Publishers.

Adam Small: "What abou' de Lô?" is reprinted from Stephen Gray, ed., *The Penguin Book of Southern African Verse* (London: Penguin Books, 1998). Used by permission of the author.

Benedict W. Vilakazi: "Umamina" is reprinted from Peggy Rutherford, ed., *African Voices: An Anthology of Native African Writing* (New York: Vanguard Press, 1960).

Patricia Jabbeh Wesley: "Nyanken Hne" and "Surrender" are reprinted from *Before the Palm Could Bloom: Poems of Africa* (Kalamazoo, Mich.: New Issues Press, 1998). Used by permission of the author.

Dan Wylie: "Loving This Younger Woman," "Loving This Older Woman," and "Ending It" are reprinted from *The Road Out* (Plumstead, Cape Town: Snailpress, 1996). Used by permission of the author.

Contributors

Abderrahim Afarki was born in 1956 in Khemisset, Morocco. In 1976, as a high school student, he was arrested for his membership in a banned organization and subsequently condemned to a ten-year prison sentence in the notorious Kenitra Central Prison. Following his release in 1987, he worked for a few years in Fes, but police harassment and surveillance forced him into exile. He was granted political refugee status in France, and he is now a French citizen, working as a librarian at the University of Paris-Sorbonne.

Mririda n'Aït Attik was born in Megdaz, a Berber village in the beautiful Tassaout valley of the Atlas Mountains of Morocco. Dubbed the Moroccan Sappho, she was famous during World War II as a courtesan-poet-singer in the *souk* of Azilal, Morocco. Her songs, composed in the Berber dialect of *tachel-hait* and based on oral traditions, were collected and translated into French by René Euloge, a French soldier who had frequented Mririda's house. After the war, she vanished from Azilal and was never heard from again. Daniel Halpern, with the help of Paula Paley, translated *The Songs of Mririda* (1974). Some of these song-poems have appeared in *The Other Voice: Twentieth-Century Women's Poetry in Translation* (1976), *Women Poets of the World* (1983), and *The Penguin Book of Women Poets* (1986).

Lounis Aït-Menguellet was born in 1950 at Aït-Badrar in Ighil Bouammas in the Djurdjura Mountains, Algeria, and is perhaps the best-known Kabyle poet/singer.

Among his early songs centered on love are "Thalt Ayam" and "Tayri." The most dynamic singer in his home area, he has become a symbol for Kabyle cultural nationalism. His poems, composed in his native Tamazight language, have been published in English translation in the *Literary Review*.

Ifi Amadiume was born in 1947 in Nigeria, where she received her early education before she went to study in England. A full professor in the Department of Religion at Dartmouth College in New Hampshire, she has also made a significant mark on African poetry. One of the most gifted and eloquent African women poets, her poetry books include *Passion Waves* (1985), *Ecstasy* (1995), *Circles of Love* (2006), and *Voices Draped in Black* (2007). Her poems have been published in numerous anthologies, including *The Heinemann Book of African Women's Poetry* (1995).

Kofi Awoonor was born in 1935 in Wheta, Ghana. Poet, university professor, and diplomat, Awoonor is among the most important African literary artists. His works include the volumes of poetry *Rediscovery* (1964), *Night of My Blood* (1971), *Come Back Ghana* (1972), *Ride Me, Memory* (1973), *South of the Sahara* (1975), *The House by the Sea* (1978), *Until the Morning After* (1987), and *Comes the Voyager at Last* (1992); translations of Ewe oral poetry, *Guardians of the Scared Word* (1974); a novel, *This Earth, My Brother* (1972); and a book of essays, *The Breast of the Earth: A Survey of the History, Culture and Literature South of the Sahara* (1976). Former Ghanaian ambassador to Cuba, Brazil, and the United Nations and minister of state in the government of Ghana, he is currently Writer in Residence at the University of Ghana, Legon.

Gabeba Baderoon was born in 1969 in Cape Town, South Africa, and grew up in Crawford, Athlone. She attended Livingstone High School in Claremont before entering the University of Cape Town, where she earned her Ph.D. in English. She also studied creative writing at Sheffield Hallam University in England and at Pennsylvania State University. Baderoon's poetry has appeared in *New Contrast*, *Carapace*, *Chimurenga*, *Illuminations*, and many other journals. She received the DaimlerChrysler Award for South African Poetry (2004), and her winning volume was published as *Museum of Ordinary Life* (2005). Her other volumes of poetry are *The Dream in the Next Body* (2005) and *A Hundred Silences* (2006).

Juma Bhalo (also known as Ahmad Nassir Juma and Ahmad Nassir bin Juma Bhalo) was born in 1937 in Mombasa, Kenya, where he currently lives and acts as sustainer of the classical traditions of Swahili poetry. He attended the Arab Boys' School, later renamed the Arab Primary School, and was educated only up to Standard IV, the equivalent of middle school. During the 1960s, he lived in Malindi but later returned to live in Old Town (Muji wa Kale), Mombasa, where he was employed as a sign painter at the docks. An accomplished calligrapher and painter, he is one of the most respected living Swahili poets.

Syl Cheney-Coker, a descendant of Creole freedmen who returned to Africa from the United States, was born Syl Cheney Coker (changing his name to its current form in 1970) in 1945 in Free Town, Sierra Leone. Poet, novelist, and journalist, he has spent a great deal of time in exile as a student in the United States. From 1966, he studied at the University of California, Los Angeles; the University of Oregon; and the University of Wisconsin–Madison. After a brief return to Sierra Leone, Cheney-Coker accepted a teaching position at the University of the Philippines, where he met his late wife, Dalisay. He has also taught at the University of Maiduguri in northern Nigeria and has been a Writer-in-Residence at the University of Iowa. His books include the poetry volumes *The Road to Jamaica* (1969), *Concerto for an Exile: Poems* (1973), *The Graveyard Also Has Teeth* (1980), and *The Blood in the Desert's Eyes: Poems* (1990) and the novel *The Last Harmattan of Alusine Dunbar* (1990). He has also edited the *Vanguard*, a progressive newspaper, in Free Town, exposing himself to death threats serious enough to cause another spate of exile.

Frank M. Chipasula, whose roots spread over much of southern Africa, extending to ancient Timbuktu, Mali, was born in 1949. He earned his undergraduate degree from the University of Zambia before studying at Brown and Yale for his two master's degrees and a Ph.D. in English literature. He has edited several anthologies of African poetry, including *The Heinemann Book of African Women's Poetry* (1995, with his wife, Stella) and *When My Brothers Come Home: Poems from Central and Southern Africa* (1985), and published volumes of his own poetry, *Visions and Reflections* (1972), *O Earth, Wait for Me* (1984), *Nightwatcher, Nightsong* (1986), *Whispers in the Wings* (1991; rpt. 2007), and *On the Shoulders of the Mountain* (2007), a poetry CD. Several of his poems have been translated into French, Chinese, and Spanish. Currently a Judge William Holmes Cook Professor at Southern Illinois University, he lives in rural southern Illinois with his wife and daughter.

Siriman Cissoko was born in 1934 in Mali but lived in Senegal. He died in 2005 at the age of seventy-one. His book-length poem, *Ressac de nous-même: poèmes* (1967), an excerpt of which appears in this anthology, is a major poetic statement on love and self-affirmation by a second-generation Malian poet. His poetry, like Léopold Sédar Senghor's, evoking the music of the Kora, celebrates his double love of the black woman and the land in a very sensuous, original, and understatedly powerful language. His second book, *Le conte du pain rassis*, was published in 1972. A few of his poems have appeared in English in Wole Soyinka's anthology, *Poems of Black Africa* (1975), and in Spanish translation elsewhere.

José Craveirinha, recognized as Mozambique's greatest poet, was born in 1922 and died in 2003 in Maputo, where he worked first as a journalist for *O Brado Africano*, *Noticias*, and *Tribuna*. In 1966, he was arrested by the Portuguese colonial authorities and imprisoned in Machava, where he was subjected to constant torture for his participation in the African resistance movements. After Mozambique's independence from Portugal, he worked as a librarian at Eduardo Mondlane University in Maputo. His many books of poetry include *Chigubo* (1964), *Karingana ua Karingana* (1974), *Cela I* (1980), and *Maria* (elegies for his wife, 1988). His poems appear in many anthologies of African poetry.

David Diop was born in 1927 in Bordeaux, France, to Senegalese and Cameroonian parents. He spent many years in poor health and was usually hospitalized, shuttling between France and Senegal. During one such trip, on August 25, 1960, he, then thirty-three; his wife, Virginie Kamara, whom he celebrates in his poem "Rama Kam"; and his second collection of poems perished off the coast of Dakar in a plane crash. The most powerful of the second generation of Negritude poets, Diop wrote an intensely erotic love poem for his wife. At his death, Diop left a single volume of his poems, *Coup de Pilon*, published in 1956. His poems appear in numerous anthologies of African poetry.

Isobel Dixon was born in 1969 in Umtata, Transkei, South Africa; grew up in the Karoo; and studied in Stellenbosch, South Africa, and Edinburgh, Scotland. Her poetry has been widely published in South Africa, where her collection *Weather Eye* (2001) won the Sanlam Prize (2000) and the Olive Schreiner Prize (2004). Internationally, her work has been published in the *Paris Review, Leviathan Quarterly, Wasafiri*, the *Guardian, London Magazine*, and the *Tall Lighthouse Review*, among others, and has been translated into German, Dutch, and Turkish. Her poems have also appeared on the Oxfam *Life Lines* CD, in the *Unfold* pamphlet (2002), and in the British Council *New Writing* anthologies. Her new collection, *A Fold in the Map* (2007), will appear in a South African edition from Jacana. She currently lives in Cambridge, works in London as a literary agent, and gives regular poetry readings.

Emanuel Dongala (Boundizeki) is a scientist, poet, and novelist who was born in 1941 in the Congo Republic. He was educated partly in the Congo and in France, where he studied the physical sciences. Upon his return to his country, he held important academic and administrative positions in the university until the civil war forced him and his family to flee to the United States with the assistance of such American and African writers as John Updike and Chinua Achebe. His poetry has been published in many international reviews and such anthologies as the *Nouvelle somme de poesie du monde noir*, edited by Paolin Joachim (1966), and Gerald Moore and Ulli Beier's *Penguin Book of Modern African Poetry* (1998).

His novel, *Un fusil dans la main, un poeme dans la poche*, was published in 1973. Since then, he has published *The Fire of Origins* (1987) and *Little Boys Are from the Stars* (1998). A holder of two doctoral degrees in the sciences, Dongala teaches at Simons Rock College of Bard College in Massachusetts.

Reesom Haile was born in 1946 in Eritrea and died in 2003. Regarded as Eritrea's poet laureate, he returned to that country in 1994 after a twenty-year exile that included teaching communications at the New School for Social Research and serving as development communications consultant for U.N. agencies, international nongovernmental organizations, and foreign governments. Committed to his mother tongue, Tigrinya, he published *Waza ms Qum Neger nTensae Hager* (1997), which won the 1998 Raimok Prize, Eritrea's highest literary award. His second volume of poems in Tigrinya is *Bahlna Bahlbana*. His other books of poetry include *We Have Our Voice: Selected Poems of Reesom Haile* (2000) and *We Invented the Wheel* (2002). His work has been translated into ten languages.

Beyene Hailemariam was born in 1955 in Eritrea. Educated in Italy, he holds a master's degree in sociology. During his nine years of incarceration in Addis Ababa, Ethiopia, he wrote some of the poems, including "Silas" and "Let's Divorce and Get Married Again," that were first published in 2000. His work appears in *Who Needs a Story? Contemporary Eritrean Poetry in Tigrinya, Tigre and Arabic*, edited by Charles Cantalupo and Ghirmai Negash (2005).

Naana Banyiwa Horne was born in 1949 in Kumasi, Ghana. She obtained a B.A. (Honors) in English and education from the University of Cape Coast in Ghana, an M.A. in English from the University of Florida, Gainesville, and a Ph.D. in African languages and literature from the University of Wisconsin–Madison. She taught at Indiana University, Kokomo, before moving to Santa Fe Community College, Gainesville, where she is currently an associate professor of English. She lives in Gainesville with her three children. An active scholar, teacher, and literary critic, she has contributed to major publications on African literature. Her poems have appeared in *Asili: The Journal of Multicultural Heartspeak*, *Santa Fe Review*, *Obsidian II: Black Literature in Review*, *The New African Poetry: An Anthology*, and her own volumes, *Sunkwa: Clingings onto Life* (1999) and *Sunkwa Revisited* (2007).

Ahmad Basheikh Husein was born in 1909 in Mombasa, Kenya, where he died in 1961. He was the greatest poet of Mombasa after the great Muyaka, though his poetry was never published during his lifetime. However, Husein recited his poems to his nephew, poet Juma Bhalo, who committed them to memory and transcribed them. Jan Knappert has preserved Husein's love songs in *Four Centuries of Swahili Verse: A Literary History and Anthology* (1979).

Rashidah Ismaili was born in 1941 in Cotonou, Benin. First educated in a Quranic school developed and headed by her maternal grandmother, she went to France and Italy to elude her Nigerian father's attempt to marry her off. She subsequently chose her own husband, from whom she is divorced. She holds a B.A. in music (voice) from the New York College of Music and an M.A. in social psychology and a Ph.D. in psychology from the New School for Social Research in New York. She is a retired professor after years of teaching at Rutgers University in New Jersey. Her books of poetry include *Oniybo and Other Poems* (1985), *Missing in Action and Presumed Dead* (1992), and *Cantata for Jimmy* (2003). Ismaili lives in Harlem, where she also has a salon-gallery that showcases writers and visual artists of color.

António Jacinto (do Amaral Martins) was born in 1924 in Luanda, Angola, and died there in 1991. He was active in the cultural movements that led to the formation of the Movimento Popular de Libertação de Angola (MPLA). He fought on the eastern front and served in the government of independent Angola under António Agostinho Neto. His poems have appeared in Mario Pinto de Andrade's anthologies, *When Bullets Begin to Flower* (1972), *No Reino de Caliban* (1975), *When My Brothers Come Home: Poems from Central and Southern Africa* (1985), and in his own volumes, *Poemas* (1961), *Outra vez Vovo Bartolomeu* (1979), and *Sobroviver em Tarrafal de Santiago* (1985), a poetic record of his fourteen-year experience in Tarrafal Prison.

David Kerr was born in 1942 in Carlisle, England, but has lived in southern Africa for much of his adult life, mainly in Malawi. He was educated in Newcastle upon Tyne, London, and obtained his Ph.D. from the University of Budapest, Hungary. A founding member of the Writers Group at Chancellor College, University of Malawi, where he taught for many years, his literary publications include a poetry chapbook, *Firstprint* (1968); *Tangled Tongues* (2003) and single poems; and short science fiction in anthologies and journals. Currently a professor at the University of Botswana, he has also taught at the universities of Malawi and Zambia. He has dedicated his life to rural community development through traveling theater.

Saba Kidane was born in 1978. Poet, performer, and journalist as well as presenter and coordinator of broadcasts on Eritrean television and radio, she also writes for newspapers. Her provocative poem "Go Crazy Over Me" resonates with the audacious and erotic poems of Mririda, the Berber courtesan poet from Morocco. Her work has been included in Charles Cantalupo and Ghirmai Negash's anthology *Who Needs a Story? Contemporary Eritrean Poetry in Tigrinya, Tigre and Arabic* (2005).

Daniel P. Kunene was born in 1923 at Edenville, Orange Free State, in South Africa. He obtained his B.A. in African languages and linguistics from the University of South Africa in 1949, later earning both his M.A. and Ph.D. degrees from the University of Cape Town, where he began his long academic career, lecturing in Bantu languages. In 1999 he was awarded the honorary degree of D. Litt. et. Phil. by his alma mater, the University of South Africa. In exile since 1963, he has taught in many African and American universities, including the University of Wisconsin–Madison, where he is professor emeritus. A staunch advocate of African-language literatures whose own poetry is deeply rooted in his native Sesotho folk literary tradition, he has translated Sesotho literature into English, and developed new approaches to the study of Africa's indigenous literatures. He not only undertook a translation of Thomas Mofolo's *Chaka* but also published two important studies on that Mosotho writer: *The Works of Thomas Mofolo: Summaries and Critiques* (1967) and *Thomas Mofolo and the Emergence of Written Sesotho Prose* (1989). A fine poet with a great sense of humor, Kunene's volumes of poetry include *Pirates Have Become Our Kings* (1978) and *A Seed Must Seem to Die* (1981), a monument to the 1976 Soweto Uprising. His hardhitting and witty stories have been collected in a volume entitled *From the Pit of Hell to the Spring of Life* (1986). Though he currently lives and writes in Madison, he actively travels and lectures.

Liyongo Fumo, whose name in translation means "Earth Spear," was a Swahili national hero who is reputed to have lived in Shaga or Shanga between 1580 and 1690. Liyongo is accredited with the invention of the *gungu* dance songs still performed at weddings and of trochaic meter, which liberated Swahili poetry from the "restrained rhythm of the religious hymns," as Jan Knappert asserts.

Lindiwe Mabuza was born in 1938 in Newcastle, Natal Province, South Africa. She obtained a B.A. from the University of Botswana, Lesotho, and Swaziland, Roma, an M.A. in American studies from the University of Minnesota, and another in literature from Stanford University. She has taught at Ohio University and at the University of Minnesota. She served as an ANC representative in Europe and Zambia during the struggle for South Africa's freedom. Active in the women's movement, she coedited an anthology, *Malibongwe: ANC Women: Poetry Is Also Their Weapon*, in 1978. Selections of her poems have appeared in Anta Sudan Katara Mberi and Cosmo Pierterse's anthology *Speak Easy, Speak Free* (1977), Barry Feinberg's anthology *Poets to the People: South African Freedom Poems* (1974; expanded ed. 1980), and *The Heinemann Book of African Women's Poetry* (1995). Her collections of poetry include *Letter to Letta* (1991), *Voices That Lead: Poems, 1976–1996* (1998), and *Footprints and Fingerprints* (2008). After having served in the same capacity in Malaysia and the Philippines, she is currently South Africa's High Commissioner to the United Kingdom.

Kristina Masuwa-Morgan (also Kristina Rungano) was born in 1963 in Harare, but she grew up in Kuatama, Zimbabwe, where she received her early education. She holds a Ph.D. in business information technology systems and is currently senior lecturer and director of the Business Information Management program at the Canterbury Christ Church University in Kent. The first and best published Zimbabwean woman poet, her books include *A Storm Is Brewing* (1984) and *To Seek a Reprieve and Other Poems* (2004). Individual poems have appeared in *Daughters of Africa* (1992), *The Heinemann Book of African Women's Poetry* (1995), *Uncommon Wealth: An Anthology of Poetry in English* (1998), *The Penguin Book of Modern African Poetry* (1998), and *Step into a World: A Global Anthology of the New Black Literature* (2000), as well as in journals.

Makhokolotso K. A. Mokhomo became the first published Mosotho woman poet when her first book of poems, *Sebabatso*, came out in 1958, although it had been ready by 1953. "When He Spoke to Me of Love," extracted from a long poem, "Muratuwa—Lerato la me," first appeared in *The Penguin Book of South African Verse* (1968).

Lupenga Mphande was born in 1947 in Thoza Village, Malawi. He was educated at the universities of Malawa, Lancaster, and Texas–Austin, where he obtained his Ph. D. in linguistics. One of Malawi's leading poets and founders of the Malawi Writers Group at the University of Malawi, he has published *A Crackle at Midnight* (1998), his first volume of poems. He has also contributed to such international poetry anthologies as *When My Brothers Come Home: Poems from Central and Southern Africa* (1985) and *The Heinemann Book of African Poetry in English* (1991) and to *Allusions, The Gar, The Kenyon Review, Poetry International, Poetry Review, West Africa,* and other journals. A tenured associate professor in the Department of African and African American Studies at Ohio State University, Columbus, he lives with his family outside of Columbus.

Muyaka bin Haji (al Ghassaniy), the most prominent early-nineteenth-century Swahili poet, who is often simply referred to as Muyaka, was born in Mombasa, Kenya, in 1776 and died in 1837. He frequently employed double-edged metaphors in his lyrical and satirical poetry, thus making it among the most complex and rich in Swahili poetry. Considered the greatest Swahili poet, Muyaka is the originator of the secular poetic tradition in Swahili. Muyaka ("handsome") was a shrewd businessman who owned several ships and made his fortune in the maritime trade.

Mvula ya Nangolo, descendant of King Nangolo, was born in 1943 in Oniimwandi Village, Uukwambi District, in northern Namibia. An accomplished journalist, he worked for two major radio stations in Central Europe, helped to launch *The Namibian Hour* on Radio Tanzania, Dar es Salaam, and later was employed as commentator, producer, and news reader for Radio Zambia in Lusaka. He also worked for the Department of Information and Publicity while editing *Namibia-Today*, the official organ of the South West People's Organization (SWAPO) in Lusaka. The first Namibian poet to write in English, his poetry volumes include *From Exile* (1976), *Thoughts from Exile* (1991), and *Watering the Beloved Desert* (2008). Individual poems have appeared in the anthologies *When My Brothers Come Home: Poems from Central and Southern Africa* (1985) and *The Penguin Book of Modern African Poetry* (1998). Highly esteemed as Namibia's national poet, he is currently special advisor to the Minister of Information and Communication Technology in Windhoek, Namibia.

António Agostinho Neto was born in 1922 in Kaxikane Village, Catete District, in the Icolo e Bengo region, about forty miles from Luanda, Angola. He studied medicine in Lisbon and Coimbra. On graduation day, he married Maria Eugenia, whom he met at university, and returned home to Angola to practice medicine. His election as president of the MPLA, the main anti-colonial movement in Angola, exposed him to Portuguese police brutality, humiliation, and imprisonment. Undaunted, he escaped from prison in Portugal and returned to lead the armed liberation struggle for Angola's independence from Portugal, becoming the new nation's first president in 1976. Although he wrote protest poems during the liberation struggle, he also left a few love poems that he wrote to Maria Eugenia from various political prisons. His poems are collected in *Sacred Hope* (1974), his sole book of poems, and he is internationally renowned as one of the most important Lusophone African poets. In 1979, Neto died in a Moscow hospital, after a prolonged illness.

Gabriel Okara was born in 1921 in Bumoundi, River Nun, the Niger Delta region in Bayelsa State, Nigeria. Okara's poems were published as *The Fisherman's Invocation* (1978), co-winner of the 1979 Commonwealth Poetry Prize, which—along with his novel, *The Voice* (1964)—marked him as one of the most linguistically innovative English-language African writers. The loss of the veteran Nigerian poet's manuscripts during the Biafran War remains a great tragedy to African literature.

Mohammed Said Osman was born in 1967. Poet and journalist, he heads the Program Development Unit for Educational Mass Media at the Ministry of Education in Eritrea. Winner of the 1995 Raimok Prize for Tigre literature, he wrote the poem "Juket" in 2000 and published *Atrafie Wo Neweshi*, a children's book in Tigre, in 2003.

Niyi Osundare was born in 1947 in Ikere-Ekiti, Nigeria. He holds a B.A. (Honors) from the University of Ibadan, an M.A. from Leeds University, and a Ph.D. from York University in Canada. Among his many books of poetry are *Songs of the*

Marketplace (1983); *Village Voices* (1984); *The Eye of the Earth* (1986), winner of the Commonwealth Poetry Prize; *Moonsongs* (1988); *Midlife* (1993); *Waiting Laughters* (1990), which won the Noma Award for Publishing in Africa; *Selected Poems* (1992); and *Pages from the Book of the Sun: New and Selected Poems* (2002). His poems have been translated into French, Dutch, Spanish, Japanese, and Korean. Following a successful career as full professor and head of the English department at the University of Ibadan, he relocated to Louisiana, where he is currently a tenured full professor of English, African, and African American literature at the University of New Orleans.

Jean-Joseph Rabéarivelo was born in 1901 in Antananarivo, Madagascar's capital, and committed suicide in 1937, at the peak of his literary powers. Partly educated by his uncle, he later attended the Ecole des Frères des Ecoles Chrétiennes at Andohalo and the Collège Saint-Michel in Amparibe. A school dropout at thirteen, he drifted from one poor-paying job to another and ended up as a printer's proofreader. Addicted to drugs and alcohol, he nevertheless read widely in the Western classics and became heavily influenced by the French symbolists and surrealists. His work is further enriched by *hain-teny*, the traditional sung poetry of the Merina people of Madagascar. He wrote fluently in both French and Spanish, publishing several volumes before his death, among them *Le Coupe de Cendres* (1924), *Sylves* (1927), *Volumes* (1928), *Presque-Songes* (1934), *Traduit de la nuit* (1935), and *Chants pour Abeone* (1937). His collection of *hain-teny*, Malagasy formalized dialogue or monologue love songs, was published posthumously as *Vieilles chansons des pays d'Imerina* in 1939. Besides French and Spanish, Rabéarivelo also composed some of his poems in his mother tongue, Hova, and translated them into French.

Jacques Rabémananjara was born in 1913 at Mangabe in Maroantsetra District, in Antongil Bay, on the east coast of Madagascar. Though he attended for the Grand Seminaire d'Antananarivo, a Jesuit college, he joined the French colonial administration. In 1939, he was sent to the French Colonial Ministry for training, but, forced to remain in France during the occupation, he studied literature at the Sorbonne. Upon his return to Madagascar, he was elected *député* in 1946, and in 1947, as a leader of the Democratic Movement for the Renewal of Madagascar, he was arrested, charged with inciting revolt against France, and sentenced to death, but his sentence was commuted to forced labor instead. A pillar of the Negritude movement, his volumes of poetry include *Sur les marches du soir* (1940), *Antidotes* (1947), *Rites millénaires* (1955), *Antsa* (1956), *Lamba* (1956), *Les ordalies* (1972), *Oeuvres complètes, poésie* (1978), *Thrènes d'avant l'aurore: Madagascar* (1985), and *Rien qu'encens et filigrane* (1987). He also published volumes of essays and plays. He served as minister and vice president of Madagascar. Following the 1972 coup d'état, he lived in Paris until his death in 2005.

Flavien Ranaivo was born in 1914 in Arivonimamo, Madagascar, and died in 1999 in Troyes, France. A love poet, he repaid his debt to the exquisite traditional *hain-teny* sung poetry of Malagasy with some of the most innovative poems in African literature. He was deeply rooted in the earth and folklore of Madagascar. For a period he was minister of information in the government. He published several volumes of his poems in French: *L'Ombre et Le Vent* (1947), *Mes Chansons de toujours* (1955), and *Le Retour au bercail* (1962).

Shaaban Robert was born in 1909 in Vibambani Village, about six miles south of Tanga, and died in 1962 in Dar es Salaam, Tanzania. Though a Yao of Mozambican and perhaps also Malawian origin, he was one of the most important modernist Swahili poets. The son of a Yao healer who migrated to Tanganyika at the early part of the twentieth century, Shaaban Robert preferred to be known as a Swahili. In 1926, following his studies at Msimbazi School in Dar es Salaam, he was among the first Tanganyikan students to pass the School Leaving Certificate Examinations and became a customs officer from 1926 to 1944. Married three times, he fathered ten children, five of whom were alive at the time of his death. Rightly called the "foster-father of Swahili" by his compatriot Matias Mnyampala, or as the *Shaha*—"king" or laureate—of modern Swahili poets, his major works include such epic poems as *Mwafrika Aimba* (1949), *Marudi Mema* (1952), and *Vita Vya Uhuru* (1967); his autobiography, *Maisha Yangu*; and *Kufikirika* (1961) and *Wasifu Wa Siti Binti Saad* (1967). He also edited the works of Mwana Kupona Msham, a major Swahili woman poet. His oeuvre consists of twenty-two books of essays, prose, and poetry, some of which have been translated into English, Russian, and Chinese. Robert was in the avant-garde of Tanganyikan writers who argued for the need to develop the Swahili language. He served on the East African Swahili Committee for many years, becoming its chairman in 1961, the year he was awarded the Margaret Wrong Memorial Prize.

David Rubadiri, pioneer Malawian poet, was born in 1930. After a long association with East Africa, he has finally returned to Malawi. After high school at Kings College, Budo, in Uganda, he studied at Makerere, Bristol, and Cambridge universities. He later taught at Makerere, Nairobi, Ife, and Gaborone. After serving his second term as Malawi's ambassador to the United Nations in New York, he became vice chancellor of the University of Malawi in Zomba until his retirement from public service in 2005. A veteran African poet whose work has appeared in numerous international journals and anthologies, Rubadiri has only recently published his poems in a single slim volume, *An African Thunderstorm and Other Poems* (2004). His anthologies include *Poems from East Africa* (1972), coedited with David Cook, and *Growing Up with Poetry* (1994). His novel, *No Bride Price* (1967), is one of the most serious fictional works from Malawi.

Tijan M. Sallah was born in 1958 in Sere Kunda, Gambia. After his secondary school education there, he studied at Berea College and the Virginia Polytechnic Institute and State University, where he was awarded a Ph.D. in economics. Following a distinguished teaching career in various U.S. universities, Sallah joined the World Bank, where he currently works. Regarded as the most significant Gambian poet after Lenrie Peters, his poetry books include *When Africa Was a Young Woman* (1980), *Kora Land* (1989), *Dreams of Dusty Roads* (1993), and *Dream Kingdom: New and Selected Poems* (2007). He has also edited and coedited *New Poets of West Africa* (1999) and, with Tanure Ojaide, *The New African Poetry* (2000).

Léopold Sédar Senghor was born in 1906 into a large family in Joal, Senegal. He was educated in Catholic mission schools in a largely Muslim country and later in Paris, where he met Aimé Césaire and Léon Damas, with whom he founded the Negritude movement, a controversial though historically important phenomenon in African literature. A member of the French Academy, he was one of the most decorated and celebrated African poets. He was both the first president of independent Senegal and the first African president to relinquish power voluntarily and peacefully when he retired on December 31, 1980, after twenty years in power. Some of his books are *Chants d'ombre* (1945), *Hostie noires* (1948), *Nocturnes* (1961), and the landmark 1948 *Anthologie de la nouvelle poesie negre et malgache*. He was also the author of the lyrics of Senegal's national anthem, "Pincez Tous vos Koras, Frappez les Balafons." He spent his last years in Normandy, France, where he died in 2001, but was buried in his village of Joal, in Senegal.

Abdul Hakim Mahmoud El-Sheikh was born in 1966 in Eritrea. Poet and journalist, he won Eritrea's Raimok Prize for Arabic poetry in 1997. One of the most promising young Eritrean poets, he died in a fire in 1998, at the height of his poetic career. "Breaths of Saffron on Broken Mirrors" was first published in 1994.

Ribka Sibhatu was born in 1956 in Eritrea. Poet, critic, and scholar with a Ph.D. in communication studies from the University of Rome, she works as an intercultural consultant in Italy, and she writes poetry in Tigrinya and Italian. "Abeba" is from her bilingual book, *Auld: Cantopoesia dall'Eritrea* (1993).

Adam Small was born in 1936 in Wellington, Cape Town, South Africa. Educated at the universities of the Western Cape, London, and Oxford, where he obtained his Ph.D. in philosophy in 1963, Small is a leading South African intellectual, poet, philosopher, and playwright. Now retired, he has taught philosophy at Fort Hare and in the School of Social Work at the University of the Western Cape. His poetic output spans the turbulent decades of apartheid, which he resisted through his poetry written in the subversive Kaaps dialect that enabled Black Afrikaans poets to reach the working-class people of the Cape and beyond. His volumes of poetry—*Verse van die liefde* (1957), *Kitaar my Kruis* (1961), *Sê sjibbolet* (1963), *Kanna hy kô hystoe* (1965), *Oos tuis bes Distrik Ses* (1973), and *Krismis van Map Jacobs* (1983)—constitute a very important seam in the rich and complex South African literary canon. He has demonstrated his versatility as a poet by writing vivid poems in both Afrikaans and English, including *Black, Bronze, Beautiful: Quatrains* (1975). His work appears in numerous journals and anthologies.

Benedict W. Vilakazi, born in 1906 at Groutville Mission in KwaZulu-Natal Province, holds the distinction of being the first black South African to be awarded the Ph.D. degree. Though named Bambatha ka Mshini, he changed his name to the current one following his family's conversion to the Roman Catholic faith. After obtaining his "candlelight" B.A. by correspondence from the University of South Africa, he became the first black South African to teach at the University of Witwatersrand. He died in 1947, soon after completing his doctoral dissertation entitled "The Oral and Written Literature of the Nguni." His literary achievements include three isiZulu language novels, though his fame rests on his two seminal volumes of poetry, *Inkondlo KaZulu* (1935) and *Amal' eZulu* (1945). Vilakazi was also an active member of the South African ANC, working closely with Chief Albert Luthuli, the first African Nobel laureate and president of the ANC; John L. Dube, the famed journalist; and others.

Patricia Jabbeh Wesley was born in Maryland County, Liberia. She was educated at the prestigious College of West Africa (high school); the University of Liberia; Indiana University, Bloomington; and Western Michigan University, where she obtained her Ph.D. in English and creative writing. Her award-winning poetry volumes include *Before the Palm Could Bloom: Poems of Africa* (1998); *Becoming Ebony* (2003), which won a 2002 Crab Orchard Award in the Second Book Poetry Open Competition; and *The River Is Rising* (2007). Her work has appeared in many literary journals and anthologies in the United States and internationally. She has lived in the U.S.A. since 1991, having fled the Liberian civil war. She currently teaches literature and creative writing at Penn State University in Altoona, Pennsylvania.

Dan Wylie was born in Bulawayo but was raised and educated in Mutare, Zimbabwe. He holds a doctorate from Rhodes University in Grahamstown, South Africa, where he is currently a lecturer in English. Winner of the 1998 Ingrid Jonker Memorial Prize for his first book of poems, *The Road Out* (1996), he has also published *Savage Delight: White Myths of Shaka* (2001), *Dead Leaves: Two Years in the Rhodesian War* (2002), and *Myth of Iron: Shaka in History* (2006).